Excel's Not Dead

William McBurnie

Grosvenor House
Publishing Limited

This book is published by
Grosvenor House Publishing Ltd
Link House
140 The Broadway, Tolworth, Surrey, KT6 7HT.
www.grosvenorhousepublishing.co.uk

A CIP record for this book
is available from the British Library

Paperback ISBN 978-1-80381-975-4
Hardback ISBN 978-1-80381-976-1
eBook ISBN 978-1-80381-977-8

Dedicated to my Family:

My Parents and Brothers and Sisters who have always supported me
and driven me to strive to be the best I can in whatever I do.

And my daughter who through her own hard work and
dedication inspires me to pursue my dreams.

For the workbooks mentioned in this book, *Worksheet 1* and *Data Dump*,
please go to www.excelsnotdead.com.

Cover art by Patrick Scantlebury

Contents

Problem Solving

I started to teach myself Excel for two main reasons. The first was that the first time I opened an Excel spreadsheet and saw what it could do I was blown away; I immediately started thinking of the time it could save me in my everyday work and the improvement in accuracy that it could create.

The second was a few years later, when it turned out that whenever I asked our "Excel Experts" for something I was told it couldn't be done when what they actually meant was they "couldn't be bothered" or they could not work out how to do it.

I do understand that for any Excel spreadsheet we are going to create we have to ask ourselves if the gains we get at the end of the day will outweigh the effort we put in; if not then we should say it is not practical or it is not an efficient use of resources, rather than it can't be done.

Over the years, I have been asked for many things that I did not know how to create so I would always say "I'll have a look" and I then take on the problem without having made any promises that I may not be able to keep.

My main concept on problem solving is to go as far as you can and get as close to the problem as possible. Some people would be asked to create something and, knowing that towards the end of the build there may be an obstacle that they do not know how to overcome, would give up then and say it can't be done. More often than not, if you were to complete the build up to the point of the obstacle, the answer would present itself once you get there.

I like to visualise it as travelling through a dense forest until you come to a clearing. Once you reach the clearing about 100 yards in front of you is the largest wall you have ever seen, it goes as far to the left and to the right as you can see and is far too high to climb. Most people, at this stage, knowing that their goal is on the other side of the wall, would give up and turn around and head back into the forest when what they should do is get as close to the obstacle as possible.

It may turn out that, as you get closer to the wall, you can see that there is a tunnel that can take you under the wall that you could not see from the forest, you may discover that there is a plastic see-through ladder so you can climb over, or even some dynamite so you can blow up the wall. None of these solutions to your problem are visible from back at the treeline, they can only be discovered if you get as close to the problem as possible.

As I am self-taught in Excel, I was fortunate enough to not have been told what I could not achieve through Excel. I always assumed that the problem was me, that everything was possible and I just had to work out how to do it. I used search engines a lot and would often end up reading questions and answers on forums about similar problems that I have had.

A prime example, and something that I still see on forums today, is the question, "How do I count colours on my spreadsheet?" and the answer is always a complicated macro that I really did not want to use (by the way, I am not bashing macros, I just know that a lot of us find them difficult, clunky and often fragile, however useful they may be). When it came to me solving the problem, again believing that everything is possible or there must be an easier way, my first thought was to see how the colours got there and what they represented. If the colours were automatically generated by conditional formatting there must be a logical condition that Excel identifies in order to apply the particular colour. If conditional formatting can identify it, so can I. Therefore, we just need to count the condition not the colour. Confused?

If your spreadsheet is measuring performance to a set target and you want to know how many of your staff are green, amber or red you just need to know what level of performance is attached to each colour and then count that with a simple formula instead of creating a macro.

Green = 100% or greater

Amber = Greater than or equal to 90% and less than 100%

Red = Less than 90%

So instead of building a macro to look for the colour green, which a normal formula cannot do, you simply build a formula to look for any percentage of 100% or greater and this will tell you the number of times that green appears on your spreadsheet.

Were they wrong to say that the only way to count colours on a spreadsheet is with a macro? No, they were absolutely right, but we don't need to count the colours to solve our actual problem.

By the way, should someone ask you to count colours that were randomly put on a spreadsheet, what would be the point? If the spreadsheet was created with no logical or consistent reason for the colours, I would give it back to the five-year-old who created it and confiscate their crayons.

As with the example above, the key is in asking the correct question, instead of necessary asking how to count colours we asked what the colours represented and counted that instead.

There is a saying that "You can't make a silk purse out of a pig's ear", which is again correct. However, you can make a purse – who said it had to be silk? (Fold ear in half and stitch down one side).

Helper Columns

I know many of us already use helper columns; my definition of them may be slightly different from other people's but I always used them when I could not get a large formula to work.

When I started, I could not get my multiple "IF" formulas to work:

	A	B	C	D
1	Student	Exam1	Exam2	Exam3
2	Adam	75.00%	80.00%	95.00%
3	Bella	40.00%	55.00%	60.00%
4	Charles	60.00%	65.00%	70.00%
5	Donna	45.00%	49.00%	50.00%
6	Ethan	25.00%	40.00%	65.00%
7	Fiona	51.00%	49.00%	70.00%

Workbook 1 Results 1

If I wanted to know which students had scored over 50% on all three exams, I would have needed the following formula in column "E":

=IF(AND(B2>50%,C2>50%,D2>50%),"Pass","Fail")

This would return "Pass" if they had or "Fail" if they had not. As at the time I could not figure out this formula or get it to work, I used helper columns to get around the problem.

	A	B	C	D	E	F	G	H	I
1	Student	Exam1	Exam2	Exam3					
2	Adam	75.00%	80.00%	95.00%	IF(B2>50%,1,0)	IF(C2>50%,1,0)	IF(D2>50%,1,0)	SUM(E2:G2)	IF(H2=3,"Pass","Fail")
3	Bella	40.00%	55.00%	60.00%					
4	Charles	60.00%	65.00%	70.00%					
5	Donna	45.00%	49.00%	50.00%					
6	Ethan	25.00%	40.00%	65.00%					
7	Fiona	51.00%	49.00%	70.00%					
8									

As I could get a single IF formula to work but not a **Multiple IF** or **IF/AND**, I put a single IF formula in each of the three helper columns, each providing a single answer, as I could not work out how to do all three at once. The formula in Column E says if the result for Exam 1 was greater than 50%, return a 1, if not, return a 0. Column F does this for the Exam 2 and Column G does this for Exam 3. This means that if all exams have a score greater than 50% there will be a 1 in E, F and G. In the next column, H, I have added E, F and G together. If the sum of E, F and G equals 3 then all three exams have been passed, so Column I says if H = 3 it's a Pass, if not it's a Fail.

Obviously, this is a long way around, but if you cannot get a single complex formula to work, break it down. It may not be silk but it's still a purse.

Conditional Formatting

Due to how I have structured this guide, this will be a very brief section on conditional formatting. It's just to give you an idea of how I approach it and why I approach it the way I do. In each of the example sections I will cover the particular conditional formatting required for that example.

Many of us find conditional formatting difficult. The section I'm talking about is the "Use a formula to decide which cells to format" section, but why is it so difficult?

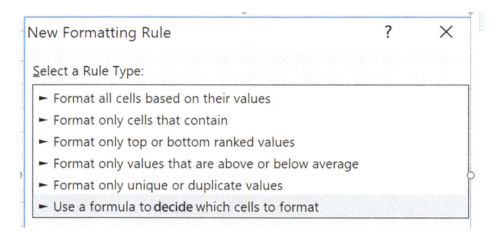

The main reason is the formulas within this section are not the same as in the rest of Excel. Conditional formatting already contains an invisible "IF" that is always at the start of any formula we create before we have started writing it, which causes a lot of confusion.

If we wanted to write a formula that in normal Excel would look like this:

=IF(A1=100%,"Green","-")

This formula basically says if cell A1 = 100% insert the word "Green" into the cell we have written the formula in, if not put in a dash.

If we wanted this in conditional formatting so it turned the whole row green, the formula we write would have to look like this:

=A1=100%

This is because conditional formatting already has the "IF(" in place at the start and the formatting you apply removes the need for the second half of the formula, so you only need the bit in the middle. Confusing, isn't it!

So knowing that formulas are harder to write in conditional formatting, I try to write all of my complex formulas for conditional formatting outside of conditional formatting and in Excel where I believe they are easier. Please bear with me.

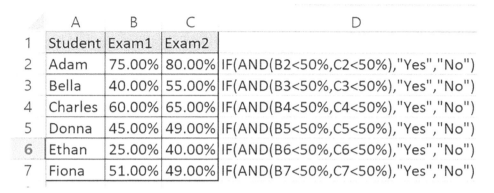

	A	B	C	D
1	Student	Exam1	Exam2	
2	Adam	75.00%	80.00%	IF(AND(B2<50%,C2<50%),"Yes","No")
3	Bella	40.00%	55.00%	IF(AND(B3<50%,C3<50%),"Yes","No")
4	Charles	60.00%	65.00%	IF(AND(B4<50%,C4<50%),"Yes","No")
5	Donna	45.00%	49.00%	IF(AND(B5<50%,C5<50%),"Yes","No")
6	Ethan	25.00%	40.00%	IF(AND(B6<50%,C6<50%),"Yes","No")
7	Fiona	51.00%	49.00%	IF(AND(B7<50%,C7<50%),"Yes","No")

Workbook 1 Results 2

(If you are not familiar with If/And formulas please refer to the Toolkit)

If I had a list of students and their results from two exams in a sheet and I wanted to highlight with conditional formatting where a student scored less than 50% in both exams, the formula in Excel would look like this:

=if(and($B2<50%,$C2<50%),"Yes","No")

This is a fairly standard formula that most of us can handle.

In conditional formatting it would look like this:

=And($B2<50%,$C2<50%)

Now for those of us who took a long time to learn how to write the first formula in Excel, to learn to leave off the front half and the back half is counter intuitive and just plain confusing, but by using a helper column within normal Excel to write the formula how we have been taught to write it and how we understand it can make the formula in conditional formatting much easier.

Because this formula in Excel (outside of conditional formatting) will return "Yes" or "No" **IF(and($B2<50%,$C2<50%), "Yes","No")** to whether or not the student failed both exams, all we then need inside conditional formatting is to select the result "Yes" or "No", and the formula is virtually complete. The formula we need in conditional formatting is:

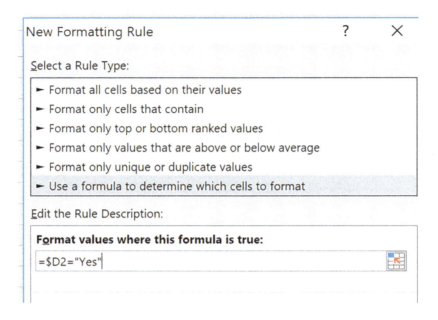

All you need to do is select the result of the Excel formula in column D and then type "="Yes"" and then set the format that you want. So Instead of:

=And($B2<50%,$C2<50%) we write:

=$D2="Yes"

This way you write your complex formulas outside of conditional formatting in Excel and keep the formulas in conditional formatting as simple as possible.

Although these are quite simple formulas you will find that you will start to use conditional formatting for more and more complex tasks because of how easy the formulas in conditional formatting will become.

The Tool Kit

In order to fully utilise my system in the following chapters we will need certain tools:

Basic Tools:

IF Formulas

Sumifs

Fixed references or $ signs

Month

Year

Rank Formulas

Data Validation\Drop down Lists

Advanced Tools:

Multiple or Nested IF Formulas

If/And Formulas

Rank Tie Breaker Formulas

Iferror Formulas

Index Match Formulas

I describe this as a toolkit because a normal toolkit does not include every tool available, just the ones that you use most often that will enable you to do 90% of your work. Your normal DIY toolkit at home may include a set of screwdrivers, a pair of plyers, a knife, and a hammer. We should be able to complete most of our DIY needs with these tools. We may need a drill of some kind from time to time but if we are not going to use it often enough could we really justify the cost or the extra effort of carrying it around?

When I go to my local DIY store they have a large saw that can cut two-meter by one-meter sheets of wood. Whilst I would love to have this in my toolkit I realise that it is way too big to carry around with me and I would only need to use it on rare occasions so cannot justify the cost or the space that it would take up. Formulas are the same.

We cannot remember every formula that is out there; if we are not using it regularly the likelihood is that we are going to forget it. This does not mean that no other formulas are useful it just means that for the purposes of following my system in this guide, this toolkit should be all you need.

An explanation of all the items in the toolkit is available in the "Toolkit Examples" section at the back of the book that will help you familiarise yourself with how the items in the toolkit work and how to use them.

If you already know all the items in the toolkit we can press on.

The Discovery

So here we go: the discovery. The main reason I came up with this discovery was because of how much I dislike pivot tables. I am not saying that pivot tables do not have their uses but I like to present my data in a particular way which usually means removing the pivot table in order to tidy up the data and if you have to do this on a regular basis you either have to write a macro to do that for you, which nobody really wants to do, or you have to create a new pivot table every time you want to reproduce that data.

What I am referring to is being able to pull out all the information for one category or type from a set of data that is in a random order as in the example below. We need to list all of the students that relate to each of the teachers in the sheet.

	A	B
1	**Teachers**	**Students**
2	Teacher 1	Adam
3	Teacher 2	Bella
4	Teacher 3	Charles
5	Teacher 1	Donna
6	Teacher 3	Etnan
7	Teacher 2	Fiona
8	Teacher 3	Michael
9	Teacher 3	Craig
10	Teacher 1	Terry
11	Teacher 3	Katrina
12	Teacher 2	Mary

Workbook 1 Teachers

If we wanted to automatically list all the students for Teacher 1 other than with a pivot table Excel would not normally be able to pull out this data with a formula like a VLOOKUP or INDEX MATCH because these formulas will only pick up the first instance of it finding the teacher we were searching for. For example, however many times we ran the following formula it would only ever return Adam for Teacher 1 and never return Donna, or Terry, or if we used a reverse lookup, it would return Terry but never Adam or Donna.

=VLOOKUP("Teacher 1",$A$2:$B$12,2,FALSE)

What we would need is a unique reference for the VLOOKUP to latch on to so it can pull in all the students that Teacher 1 has. We would normally do this in a pivot table that would need to be manually refreshed any time the data changed, but there is another way.

Rank formulas are very important in the system I use as I need to be able to search for a unique but predictable identifier in order to create my list using a lookup or index/match.

In order to achieve this alongside my data I would create a few helper columns in order to Rank my items and create my unique but predictable identifiers. To do this I would add an IF formula to my Rank to say only if the Teacher is the Teacher we are looking for should Excel complete the Rank.

	A	B	C	D
1	Teachers	Students	Ref	Teacher 1
2	Teacher 1	Adam	1	IF($A2="Teacher 1",RANK(C2,C$2:C$12),0)
3	Teacher 2	Bella	2	IF($A3="Teacher 1",RANK(C3,C$2:C$12),0)
4	Teacher 3	Charles	3	IF($A4="Teacher 1",RANK(C4,C$2:C$12),0)
5	Teacher 1	Donna	4	IF($A5="Teacher 1",RANK(C5,C$2:C$12),0)
6	Teacher 3	Etnan	5	IF($A6="Teacher 1",RANK(C6,C$2:C$12),0)
7	Teacher 2	Fiona	6	IF($A7="Teacher 1",RANK(C7,C$2:C$12),0)
8	Teacher 3	Michael	7	IF($A8="Teacher 1",RANK(C8,C$2:C$12),0)
9	Teacher 3	Craig	8	IF($A9="Teacher 1",RANK(C9,C$2:C$12),0)
10	Teacher 1	Terry	9	IF($A10="Teacher 1",RANK(C10,C$2:C$12),0)
11	Teacher 3	Katrina	10	IF($A11="Teacher 1",RANK(C11,C$2:C$12),0)
12	Teacher 2	Mary	11	IF($A12="Teacher 1",RANK(C12,C$2:C$12),0)

In column C I would create a sequential list of numbers from 1 to however far down your list goes, in this case 11.

I would then create an IF formula to rank only the numbers on the list where "Teacher 1" appears in column A:

IF($A2="Teacher 1",RANK(C2,C$2:C$12),0)

If cell A2 = "Teacher 1" Rank the number in cell C2 amongst the numbers from cell C2 to cell C12. If cell A2 does not equal Teacher 1, put a zero.

The result would look like this:

	A	B	C	D
1	Teachers	Students	Ref	Teacher 1
2	Teacher 1	Adam	1	11
3	Teacher 2	Bella	2	0
4	Teacher 3	Charles	3	0
5	Teacher 1	Donna	4	8
6	Teacher 3	Etnan	5	0
7	Teacher 2	Fiona	6	0
8	Teacher 3	Michael	7	0
9	Teacher 3	Craig	8	0
10	Teacher 1	Terry	9	3
11	Teacher 3	Katrina	10	0
12	Teacher 2	Mary	11	0

Unfortunately, this still is not enough to get us what we want as these numbers we now have in Column D are also random (11, 8 and 3) and there is no way to predict what numbers will appear as we don't know where or how many times Teacher 1 may appear in the list.

So we have to remember our problem solving and ask ourselves if there is a solution to our specific problem. What we need is a set of numbers in order so we have our unique and predictable identifiers. Do we know of a formula to sort numbers out into a predetermined order...? Yes: "Rank".

If we now add another helper column in Column E and rank the result of our first rank (Column D) the formula would look like this:

IF(D20=0,0,RANK(D2,D$2:D$12))

So if the first Rank in column D = 0 Return 0, if it doesn't Rank the number against the other numbers in column D.

	A	B	C	D	E	F	G	H
1	Teachers	Students	Ref	Teacher 1	RANK 2			
2	Teacher 1	Adam	1	11	IF(D2=0,0,RANK(D2,$D$2:$D$12))			
3	Teacher 2	Bella	2	0	IF(D3=0,0,RANK(D3,$D$2:$D$12))			
4	Teacher 3	Charles	3	0	IF(D4=0,0,RANK(D4,$D$2:$D$12))			
5	Teacher 1	Donna	4	8	IF(D5=0,0,RANK(D5,$D$2:$D$12))			
6	Teacher 3	Etnan	5	0	IF(D6=0,0,RANK(D6,$D$2:$D$12))			
7	Teacher 2	Fiona	6	0	IF(D7=0,0,RANK(D7,$D$2:$D$12))			
8	Teacher 3	Michael	7	0	IF(D8=0,0,RANK(D8,$D$2:$D$12))			
9	Teacher 3	Craig	8	0	IF(D9=0,0,RANK(D9,$D$2:$D$12))			
10	Teacher 1	Terry	9	3	IF(D10=0,0,RANK(D10,$D$2:$D$12))			
11	Teacher 3	Katrina	10	0	IF(D11=0,0,RANK(D11,$D$2:$D$12))			
12	Teacher 2	Mary	11	0	IF(D12=0,0,RANK(D12,$D$2:$D$12))			

And the result would look like this:

	A	B	C	D	E
1	Teachers	Students	Ref	Teacher 1	Rank 2
2	Teacher 1	Adam	1	11	1
3	Teacher 2	Bella	2	0	0
4	Teacher 3	Charles	3	0	0
5	Teacher 1	Donna	4	8	2
6	Teacher 3	Etnan	5	0	0
7	Teacher 2	Fiona	6	0	0
8	Teacher 3	Michael	7	0	0
9	Teacher 3	Craig	8	0	0
10	Teacher 1	Terry	9	3	3
11	Teacher 3	Katrina	10	0	0
12	Teacher 2	Mary	11	0	0

So now in column E we have a set of numbers that identify any time Teacher 1 appears and it is in a unique and predictable order: 1, 2 and 3 and would continue to go up in increments of 1 for as many times as Teacher 1 appears.

We can now create an "INDEX MATCH" formula (see the Tool kit Examples) to bring in the students in rank order as below:

=INDEX(B$2:B$12,Match($C1,E$2:E$12,0))

So we are going to bring in the student in column B (highlighted in red in the formula) where the unique rank in column E (highlighted in green in the formula) matches the first number in column C which is 1 (highlighted in blue in the formula).

	A	B	C	D	E	F	G	H	I
1	Teachers	Students	Ref	Teacher	Rank 2				
2	Teacher 1	Adam	1	11	1		INDEX(B$2:B$12,MATCH(C2,E$2:E$12,0))		
3	Teacher 2	Bella	2	0	0		INDEX(B$2:B$12,MATCH(C3,E$2:E$12,0))		
4	Teacher 3	Charles	3	0	0		INDEX(B$2:B$12,MATCH(C4,E$2:E$12,0))		
5	Teacher 1	Donna	4	8	2		INDEX(B$2:B$12,MATCH(C5,E$2:E$12,0))		
6	Teacher 3	Etnan	5	0	0		INDEX(B$2:B$12,MATCH(C6,E$2:E$12,0))		
7	Teacher 2	Fiona	6	0	0		INDEX(B$2:B$12,MATCH(C7,E$2:E$12,0))		
8	Teacher 3	Michael	7	0	0		INDEX(B$2:B$12,MATCH(C8,E$2:E$12,0))		
9	Teacher 3	Craig	8	0	0		INDEX(B$2:B$12,MATCH(C9,E$2:E$12,0))		
10	Teacher 1	Terry	9	3	3		INDEX(B$2:B$12,MATCH(C10,E$2:E$12,0))		
11	Teacher 3	Katrina	10	0	0		INDEX(B$2:B$12,MATCH(C11,E$2:E$12,0))		
12	Teacher 2	Mary	11	0	0		INDEX(B$2:B$12,MATCH(C12,E$2:E$12,0))		

And the result will look like this:

	A	B	C	D	E	F	G
1	Teachers	Students	Ref	Teacher	Rank 2		
2	Teacher 1	Adam	1	11	1		Adam
3	Teacher 2	Bella	2	0	0		Donna
4	Teacher 3	Charles	3	0	0		Terry
5	Teacher 1	Donna	4	8	2		#N/A
6	Teacher 3	Etnan	5	0	0		#N/A
7	Teacher 2	Fiona	6	0	0		#N/A
8	Teacher 3	Michael	7	0	0		#N/A
9	Teacher 3	Craig	8	0	0		#N/A
10	Teacher 1	Terry	9	3	3		#N/A
11	Teacher 3	Katrina	10	0	0		#N/A
12	Teacher 2	Mary	11	0	0		#N/A

We now have the students who are taught by Teacher 1 only in our list, which is something that most people believe Excel **cannot** do without a pivot table. But as you can see it requires some tidying up.

The Next Steps

At this stage, if you know how to apply an "IFERROR" formula you will have everything you need to create your own dynamic formulas without the need for pivot tables and therefore without the need to create macros to refresh them when the data is changed. I do, however, tend to take things a bit further in the name of neatness.

To tidy this up I would firstly wrap our last formula in column G in an "IFERROR" formula. This basically says if the result of the formula is an error do not display the error show something else instead.

When I say wrap it in the formula, that is exactly what I mean. So at the front of our already built and working formula we put the "**IFERROR(**" and at the end of our formula we put a coma, what we would like to appear instead of the error and then a close bracket (if we want text in place of an error we must enclose it in double speech marks). I have chosen to use text "No More Data".

IFERROR(INDEX(B$2:B$12,MATCH(C2,E$2:E$12,0))**,"No More Data")**

The result of which looks like this:

	A	B	C	D	E	F	G
1	Teachers	Students	Ref	Teacher	Rank 2		
2	Teacher 1	Adam	1	11	1		Adam
3	Teacher 2	Bella	2	0	0		Donna
4	Teacher 3	Charles	3	0	0		Terry
5	Teacher 1	Donna	4	8	2		No More Data
6	Teacher 3	Etnan	5	0	0		No More Data
7	Teacher 2	Fiona	6	0	0		No More Data
8	Teacher 3	Michael	7	0	0		No More Data
9	Teacher 3	Craig	8	0	0		No More Data
10	Teacher 1	Terry	9	3	3		No More Data
11	Teacher 3	Katrina	10	0	0		No More Data
12	Teacher 2	Mary	11	0	0		No More Data

Now by this stage, if this were to be my presentation sheet, I would have hidden columns A to F, leaving just column G on display (once you get used to this system you can put these calculations on a separate sheet from your presentation sheet and hide the calculation sheet altogether).

So I would end up with something like this:

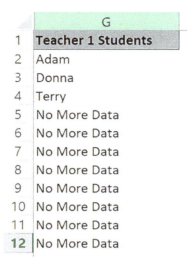

Whenever I am presenting data I like to have it wrapped in a border, the problem here is I don't really want to show where there is "No More Data" and I don't want to leave a load of blank cells as I cannot be sure how many students there are on the list for Teacher 1 so I need to use some conditional formatting.

I would select cells G2 to G12 and then open conditional formatting, then "New Rules" and "Use a formula to determine which cells to format" as below:

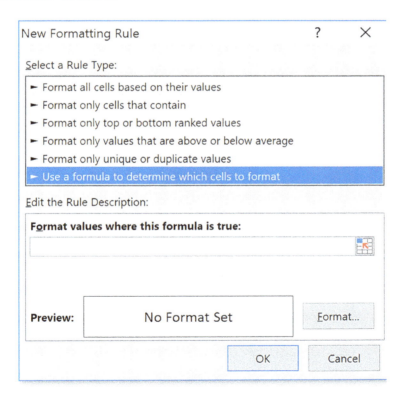

Within the format box I would input the following formula.

The first formula is going to say that if the cell G2= "No More Data" to change the font to white (so it is not visible and to remove any borders.

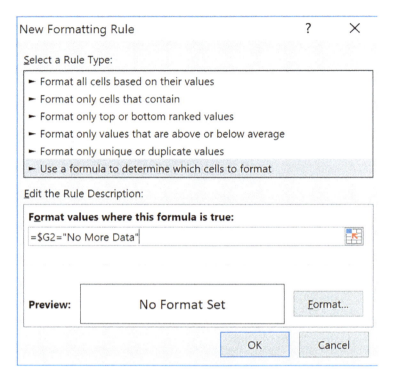

I would then select "Format", "Font" and change the colour to white.

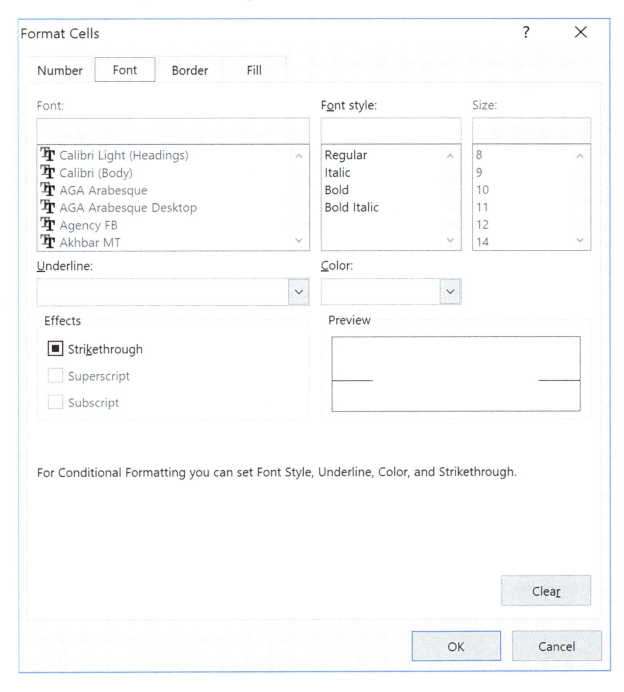

Select "Border" and from "Presets" select "None":

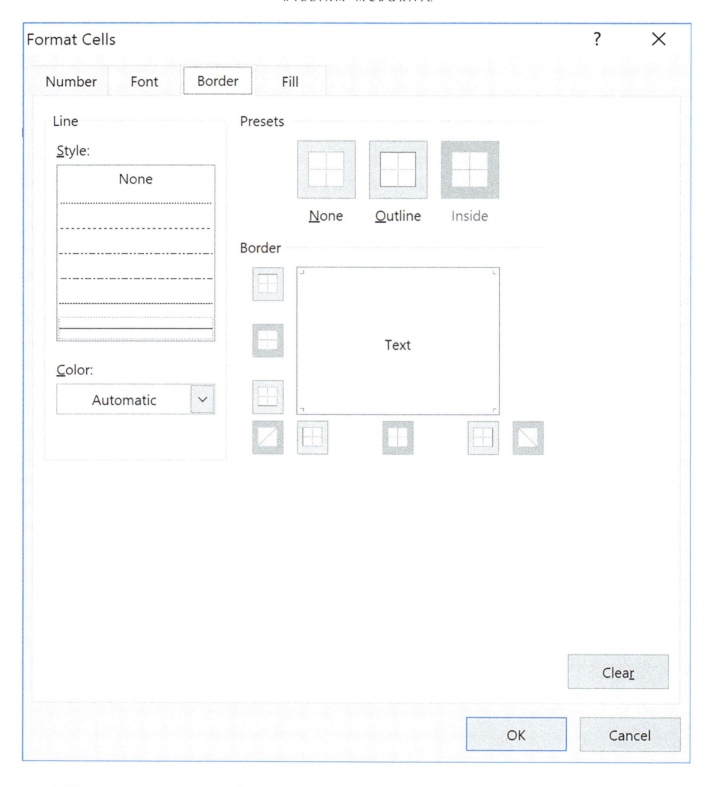

Press "OK" twice and then press "Apply":

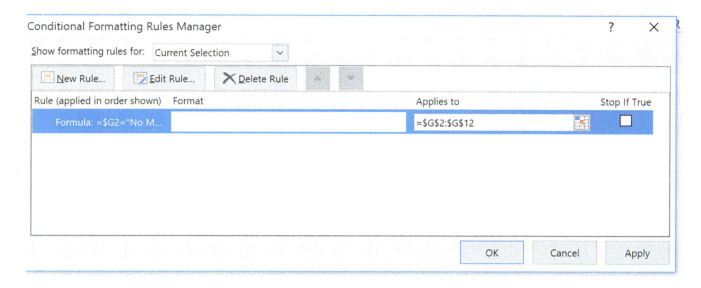

The result should look like this:

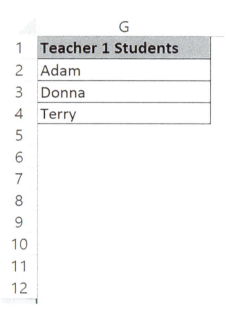

The second conditional formatting formula is applied in the same way.

I would select cells G2 to G12 and then open conditional formatting, then "New Rules" and "Use a formula to determine which cells to format" as below:

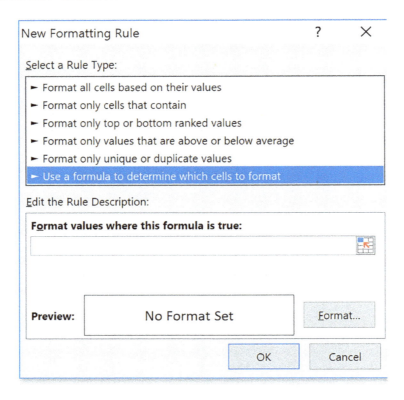

Within the format box I would input the following formula.

If the cell G2 does not equal "No More Data" to change the font to black (so it is visible) and to put all boarders in place, the opposite of the first formula.

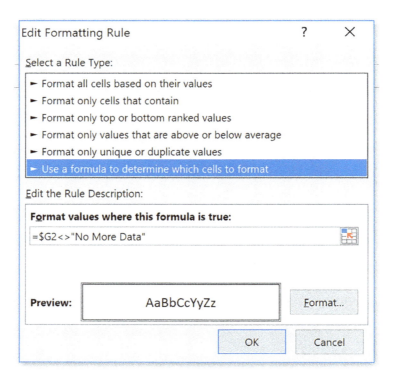

Then select "Format" and change the font colour to black:

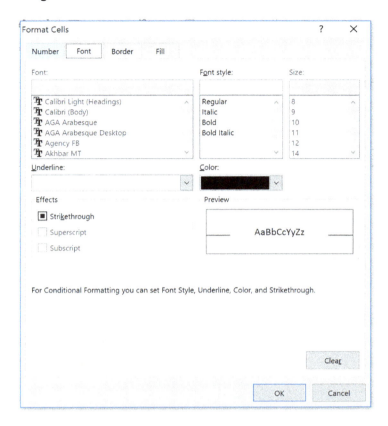

And then select "Border" and choose "Outline" from "Presets":

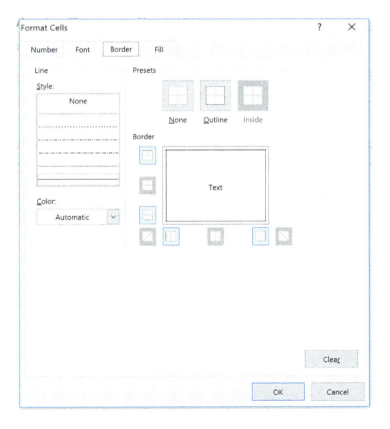

Press "OK" twice and then press "Apply":

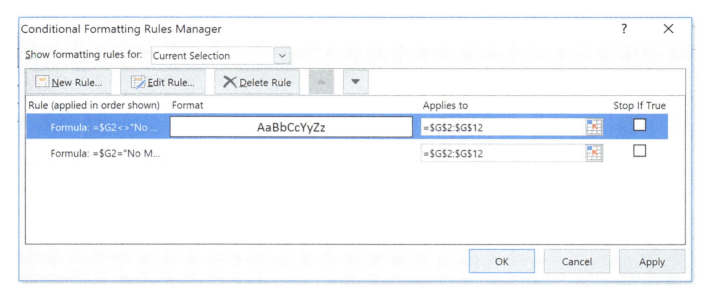

The result should look like this with cells G2 to G4 neatly wrapped in a border:

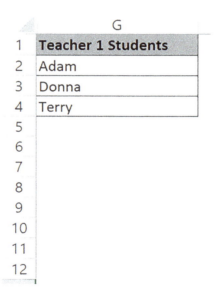

You now have a spreadsheet that will bring in only the lines of data that you want from a random sample of data where you need to return multiple results for the same criteria and will automatically wrap only the rows of data that you have.

If you were to now go back and unhide your original data and change the teacher for the student called Bella to Teacher 1 her name would now appear in column G between Adam and Donna and cells 2 to 5 will now be wrapped.

In reality, I would not have the formula in column D hardcoded with "Teacher 1". My preferred technique would be to use a dropdown or validation list with my teachers in it and link the formula directly to that as below. So I would add a few rows above our original sheet and set up the validation list in cell B2.

Instead of using the formula =**IF($A5=**"Teacher 1",**Rank(C5,C$5:C$15),0)** we replace "Teacher 1" with the validation list that we have created in cell B2:

=**IF(A5=$B$2,Rank(C5,C$5:C$15),0)**

This now makes the formula dynamic and will change the results based on the teacher selected from the validation list without having to change the formula.

	A	B	C	D
1				
2		Teacher 1		
3				
4	Teachers	Students	Ref	Teacher 1
5	Teacher 1	Adam	1	IF($A5=$B$2,RANK(C5,C$5:C$15),0)
6	Teacher 1	Bella	2	10
7	Teacher 3	Charles	3	0
8	Teacher 1	Donna	4	8
9	Teacher 3	Etnan	5	0
10	Teacher 2	Fiona	6	0
11	Teacher 3	Michael	7	0
12	Teacher 3	Craig	8	0
13	Teacher 1	Terry	9	3
14	Teacher 3	Katrina	10	0
15	Teacher 2	Mary	11	0

The last thing I would do on this project is ensure that we knew exactly what we were looking at by amending the heading on our original teacher list:

In cell G1 the heading, I would insert the formula =**B2&" Students"** (within the speech marks you need to put a space before the word "Students"). This now means that when we change the teacher in the validation list in B2, the heading will automatically update and will always show the teacher we are searching for followed by the word "Students".

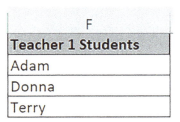

Advanced

The Double Rank system in the previous chapter has many uses, one of which would be to prepopulate fields on various worksheets in a spreadsheet. This means from a single data set you can have the students for each teacher pulling into a separate worksheet, one for each teacher.

If we keep it basic and use our list of students and teachers that we already have I would first create a separate worksheet for each of the teachers. I would normally create a "Calculation Sheet" to put my formulas in, but for ease we will put them all on the main page so we can see them all at once.

If we now use *Worksheet 1 Student Data,* I have kept the reference numbers in column C5 to 15 (or however many you need) and I have put the name of the first teacher in column D3 so we know who we are looking for. Underneath that, in D4, I have put the label "Rank1" The first formula in D5 says that if "A5" ="$D$3", Teacher 1, rank the number in C1. This is pretty much the same as our original formula but this one is looking in D3 for our teacher.

=IF(A5=$D$3,RANK($C5,$C$5:$C$15),0)

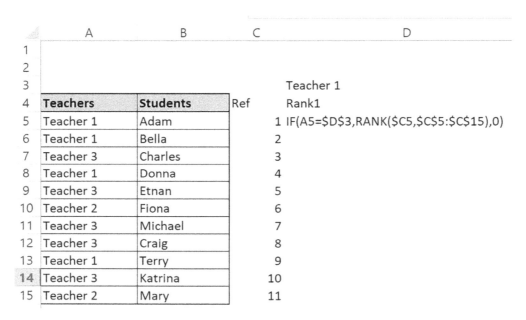

Worksheet 1 Student Data

We copy this down to row 15 to cover all the items in our sheet.

The formula in column E is exactly the same as our original second rank as below it only ranks if there is a number in the first rank not 0:

IF(D20=0,0,RANK(D2,D$2:D$12))

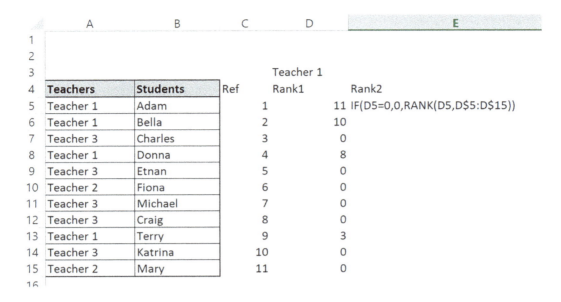

This will give us our unique and predictable pattern again of 1, 2 , 3, and so on, copy this down to row 15 to cover all our data.

We now need to repeat this for each teacher in the rows to the right, F, G, H and I, as below, remembering to change the teacher name in row 3.

So Rank 1 in column F would read:

=IF(A5=$F$3,RANK($C5,$C$5:$C$15),0)

The only thing changing would be D3 to F3 to now look for Teacher 2 and the formula would change in column H to:

=IF(A5=$H$3,RANK($C5,$C$5:$C$15),0)

If we have managed to build the formulas correctly, we will have something that looks like this (without the colours):

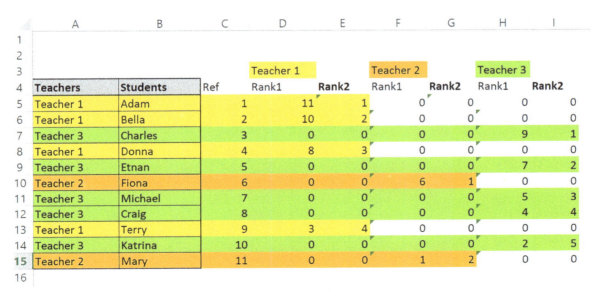

For Teacher 1 in **yellow** Rank 2 in column E identifies their students 1, 2, 3 and 4, Adam , Bella, Donna and Terry.

For Teacher 2 in **orange** Rank 2 in column G identifies their students 1 and 2, Fiona and Mary.

For Teacher 3 in **green** Rank 2 in column I identifies their students 1, 2, 3, 4 and 5, Charles, Etnan, Michael, Craig and Katrina.

Create 3 new worksheets titled Teacher 1, Teacher 2 and Teacher 3. In the Teacher 1 worksheet I would put the numbers 1 to 11 in column A starting at A2 and put a heading of Students in cell B1.

	A	B
1		**Students**
2	1	
3	2	
4	3	
5	4	
6	5	
7	6	
8	7	
9	8	
10	9	
11	10	
12		

As before we are going to need an INDEX MATCH to bring in the student's name from the Student Data sheet.

	A	B
1		**Students**
2	1	INDEX('Student Data'!B:B,MATCH('Teacher 1'!A2,'Student Data'!E:E,0))
3	2	
4	3	
5	4	
6	5	
7	6	
8	7	
9	8	
10	9	
11	10	

= INDEX('Student Data'!B:B,MATCH('Teacher 1'!A2,'Student Data'!E:E,0))

This formula is now bringing in the student name in column B of the Student Data sheet by matching the number 1 in column A of the Teacher 1 sheet in the Rank 2 Column (Column E) of the Student Data sheet.

Copy this to row 11 to cover our data. We can tidy this up with an "IFERROR" as before.

Iferror(INDEX('Student Data'!B:B,MATCH('Teacher 1'!A2,'Student Data'!E:E,0)),"No More Data")

	A	B
1		**Students**
2	1	Adam
3	2	Bella
4	3	Donna
5	4	Terry
6	5	No More Data
7	6	No More Data
8	7	No More Data
9	8	No More Data
10	9	No More Data
11	10	No More Data
12		

And then apply the conditional formatting to wrap your data and hide the "No More Errors" and hide "Column A".

And it should look like this:

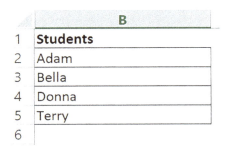

	B
1	**Students**
2	Adam
3	Bella
4	Donna
5	Terry
6	

For Teacher 2 I would copy the whole Teacher 1 worksheet and paste it into Teacher 2. The only difference between the two sheets is that instead of matching our Rank in column E:E ,the Teacher 1 Rank 2 column, we want to match in column G:G, the Teacher 2 Rank 2 column.

In order to do this I would highlight the whole Teacher 2 sheet that we have just pasted the Teacher 1 page into, go into "Find and Replace" and replace E:E with G:G.

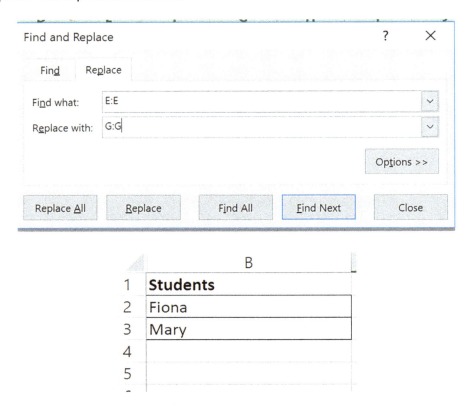

This will now automatically bring in the students for Teacher 2. If we do the same for the Teacher 3 sheet we just have to change from G:G to I:I. Easy!

So you now have three separate worksheets, one for each teacher that will automatically update independently when the data changes in the Student Data sheet and we have used no macros and no pivot tables.

Dynamic Sheets

Despite the revelation that we can create automated filters similar to pivot tables without the need for macros to refresh them, there is still a fair bit that pivot tables can do that we haven't covered.

Our new sheets using the Double Rank method can create for us bespoke sheets from data where the subject appears multiple times (Teacher 1 may have four students so would appear four times).

In the sheet below (*Worksheet 1 Dynamic Sheets*) we can see that many of the salesforce appear in our data set more than once, we need to be able to create a new sheet where anyone in the salesforce appears just once in the same way that a pivot table would but in an automated way.

Salesforce	Revenue From Sales
Adam	£601
Bella	£717
Charles	£691
Donna	£183
Etnan	£569
Fiona	£412
Michael	£74
Adam	£260
Terry	£657
Katrina	£87
Mary	£437
Adam	£854
Bella	£452
Charles	£105
Donna	£531
Etnan	£711
Fiona	£497

Worksheet 1 Dynamic Sheets

As before, we need to assign a unique number to each name the *first* time it appears in our sheet. As we need to identify *only* the first time a name appears we would create the following formula:

=IF(COUNTIF($A$2:A3,A3)=1,C2+1,C2)

Count how many times a name appears between the first name in our list and the row we are on. If the count is one, the name has only appeared once and is therefore unique so we add one to the previous number in our list creating a unique number. If the count is greater than one, the name is not unique and has appeared previously in our list so we use the previous number which is not unique.

In column C, the line with the first person in the sales force, "Adam" (cell A2), we would insert the number one as the first name in our list will always be unique as it is the first name. In the next cell down (C3), we would input the first formula which says between the range of $A$2 (a fixed reference that means our range will always start at A2) and A3 (not fixed so it will continue to move and extend our range as we copy the formula down) count how many times we see A3.

So the first section of our formula says how many times do you count "Bella" between A2 and A3.

If whatever is in A3 appears just once from A2 down then the count will be one, meaning that this is the first time we have seen this name. Where that is the case, add one to the previous cell, C2, (our base) which would give this name "Bella" a unique reference. If it does not equal one, bring in the number from the previous cell, C2, without adding one so the number stays the same.

	A	B	C
1	Salesforce	Revenue From Sales	
2	Adam	601	1
3	Bella	717	=IF(COUNTIF($A$2:A3,A3)=1,C2+1,C2)
4	Charles	691	=IF(COUNTIF($A$2:A4,A4)=1,C3+1,C3)
5	Donna	183	=IF(COUNTIF($A$2:A5,A5)=1,C4+1,C4)
6	Etnan	569	=IF(COUNTIF($A$2:A6,A6)=1,C5+1,C5)
7	Fiona	412	=IF(COUNTIF($A$2:A7,A7)=1,C6+1,C6)
8	Michael	74	=IF(COUNTIF($A$2:A8,A8)=1,C7+1,C7)
9	Adam	260	=IF(COUNTIF($A$2:A9,A9)=1,C8+1,C8)
10	Terry	657	=IF(COUNTIF($A$2:A10,A10)=1,C9+1,C9)
11	Katrina	87	=IF(COUNTIF($A$2:A11,A11)=1,C10+1,C10)
12	Mary	437	=IF(COUNTIF($A$2:A12,A12)=1,C11+1,C11)
13	Adam	854	=IF(COUNTIF($A$2:A13,A13)=1,C12+1,C12)
14	Bella	452	=IF(COUNTIF($A$2:A14,A14)=1,C13+1,C13)
15	Charles	105	=IF(COUNTIF($A$2:A15,A15)=1,C14+1,C14)
16	Donna	531	=IF(COUNTIF($A$2:A16,A16)=1,C15+1,C15)
17	Etnan	711	=IF(COUNTIF($A$2:A17,A17)=1,C16+1,C16)
18	Fiona	497	=IF(COUNTIF($A$2:A18,A18)=1,C17+1,C17)

The results once the formula has been copied down the column will look like this:

	A	B	C
1	Salesforce	Revenue From Sales	
2	Adam	£601	1
3	Bella	£717	2
4	Charles	£691	3
5	Donna	£183	4
6	Etnan	£569	5
7	Fiona	£412	6
8	Michael	£74	7
9	Adam	£260	7
10	Terry	£657	8
11	Katrina	£87	9
12	Mary	£437	10
13	Adam	£854	10
14	Bella	£452	10
15	Charles	£105	10
16	Donna	£531	10
17	Etnan	£711	10
18	Fiona	£497	10

When we get to cell C9 we notice that the number does not change and remains at 7, this is because when we count the number of times Adam appears from $A$2 (a fixed reference) to A9, the count is two so it is not the first time we have seen that name so we do not assign a new and unique number to it, instead we give it the number that is in the cell above, which is 7.

In A10, A11 and A12 we find "Terry", "Katrina" and "Mary", who all appear for the first time so they get the unique numbers 8 and 9 and 10 respectively. In cell A13, "Adam" appears again and as the number of times "Adam" appears between A2 (a fixed reference) and A13 is 3 and therefore not the first time we have seen the name so no unique number is assigned.

We are now in a position as in the previous **Discovery** chapter to use an INDEX MATCH to pick up the names using the unique references we have just created (this would normally be created in a separate sheet but for ease of display I have kept all of the formulas together).

In column D I would create a sequential list of numbers from 1 to however far down your list goes, in this case 17, and label it "Order" (in reality, I would always extend my formulas beyond the bottom of my data list to allow for more data).

Create the formula below in cell E2, which says bring in the Salesforce Name (in red A2:A18) where the Order number (in blue D2) is the same as the Unique Reference in (in green C2:C18):

=INDEX($A$2:$A$18,MATCH(D2,$C$2:$C$18,0))

	A	B	C	D	E
1	Salesforce	Revenue From Sales	Unique Ref	Order	List with Duplicates Removed
2	Adam	601	1	1	=INDEX($A$2:$A$18,MATCH(D2,$C$2:$C$18,0))
3	Bella	717	2	2	
4	Charles	691	3	3	
5	Donna	183	4	4	
6	Etnan	569	5	5	
7	Fiona	412	6	6	
8	Michael	74	7	7	
9	Adam	260	7	8	
10	Terry	657	8	9	
11	Katrina	87	9	10	
12	Mary	437	10	11	
13	Adam	854	10	12	
14	Bella	452	10	13	
15	Charles	105	10	14	
16	Donna	531	10	15	
17	Etnan	711	10	16	
18	Fiona	497	10	17	

Once the formula is copied down the results are as below:

	A	B	C	D	E
1	Salesforce	Revenue From Sales	Unique Ref	Order	List with Duplicates Removed
2	Adam	£601	1	1	Adam
3	Bella	£717	2	2	Bella
4	Charles	£691	3	3	Charles
5	Donna	£183	4	4	Donna
6	Etnan	£569	5	5	Etnan
7	Fiona	£412	6	6	Fiona
8	Michael	£74	7	7	Michael
9	Adam	£260	7	8	Terry
10	Terry	£657	8	9	Katrina
11	Katrina	£87	9	10	Mary
12	Mary	£437	10	11	#N/A
13	Adam	£854	10	12	#N/A
14	Bella	£452	10	13	#N/A
15	Charles	£105	10	14	#N/A
16	Donna	£531	10	15	#N/A
17	Etnan	£711	10	16	#N/A
18	Fiona	£497	10	17	#N/A

We now have a dynamic sheet that will automatically remove the duplicates from any given list. So we can see that our new list only has one of each of our salesforce. As in our previous chapter, we need to tidy up our sheet with an IFERROR and some conditional formatting.

=IFERROR(INDEX($A$2:$A$18,MATCH(D2,$C$2:$C$18,0)),"No More Data"

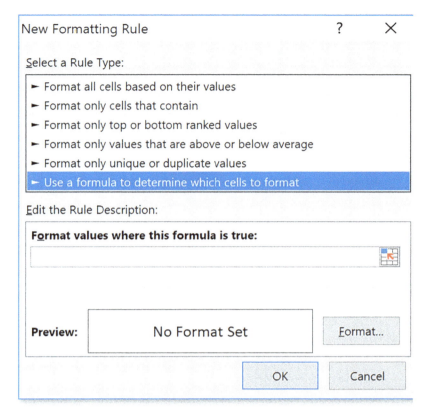

Within the format box, I would input the following formula.

The first formula is going to say that if the cell E2= "No More Data" to change the font to white (so it is not visible and to remove any borders).

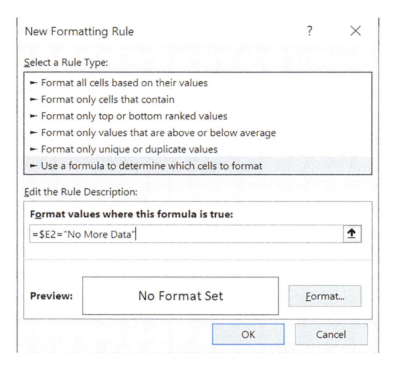

I would then select "Format" and "Font" then change the colour to white.

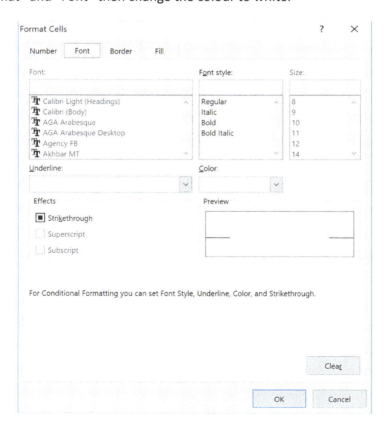

Select "Border" and select "None" from presets.

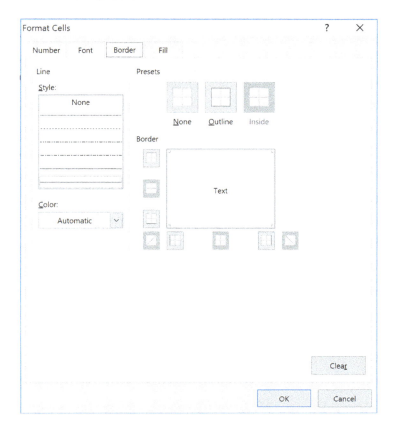

Press "OK" twice and then select "Apply":

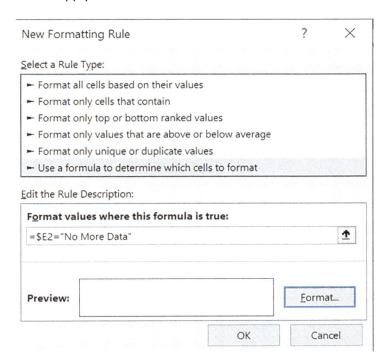

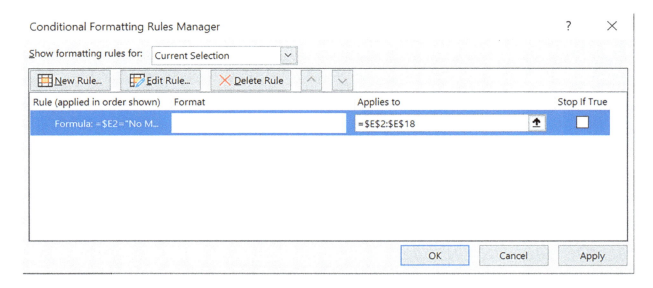

Then, as before, apply the conditional formatting for if E2 does not equal "No More Data":

=$E2<>"No More Data" as in the Discovery chapter and the results would be as below:

List with Duplicates Removed
Adam
Bella
Charles
Donna
Etnan
Fiona
Michael
Terry
Katrina
Mary

From here we can build out our automated sheet to bring in the revenue for each member of the salesforce.

As we do not wish to lose the additional data where the salesforce appears more than once, we can use a standard SUMIFS formula in column F:

=SUMIFS($B$2:$B$18,$A$2:$A$18,$E2)

	A	B	C	D	E	F
1	Salesforce	Revenue From Sales	Unique Ref	Order	List with Duplicates Removed	Revenue from Sales
2	Adam	601	1	1	Adam	=SUMIFS($B$2:$B$18,$A$2:$A$18,$E2)
3	Bella	717	2	2	Bella	=SUMIFS($B$2:$B$18,$A$2:$A$18,$E3)
4	Charles	691	3	3	Charles	=SUMIFS($B$2:$B$18,$A$2:$A$18,$E4)
5	Donna	183	4	4	Donna	=SUMIFS($B$2:$B$18,$A$2:$A$18,$E5)
6	Etnan	569	5	5	Etnan	=SUMIFS($B$2:$B$18,$A$2:$A$18,$E6)
7	Fiona	412	6	6	Fiona	=SUMIFS($B$2:$B$18,$A$2:$A$18,$E7)
8	Michael	74	7	7	Michael	=SUMIFS($B$2:$B$18,$A$2:$A$18,$E8)
9	Adam	260	7	8	Terry	=SUMIFS($B$2:$B$18,$A$2:$A$18,$E9)
10	Terry	657	8	9	Katrina	=SUMIFS($B$2:$B$18,$A$2:$A$18,$E10)
11	Katrina	87	9	10	Mary	=SUMIFS($B$2:$B$18,$A$2:$A$18,$E11)
12	Mary	437	10	11		
13	Adam	854	10	12		
14	Bella	452	10	13		
15	Charles	105	10	14		
16	Donna	531	10	15		
17	Etnan	711	10	16		
18	Fiona	497	10	17		

This will simply add together the revenue from sales for each member of the salesforce.

List with Duplicates Removed	Revenue from Sales
Adam	£1,715.00
Bella	£1,169.00
Charles	£796.00
Donna	£714.00
Etnan	£1,280.00
Fiona	£909.00
Michael	£74.00
Terry	£657.00
Katrina	£87.00
Mary	£437.00

Now, just like a pivot table, we would need to add a formula to generate a dynamic total at the bottom of our sheet so that, regardless of how many items there are in our sheet, our total will always be on the cell under the last line of information (where it should be).

Once again, most of these helper columns would be put in a separate sheet but for ease I will put them on the same page.

Firstly, I would create a helper column that exactly repeats column E, the "List with Duplicates Removed" column, in column G, as below:

IFERROR(INDEX($A$2:$A$18,MATCH($D2,$C$2:$C$18,0)),"No More Data")

We need to do this as in the next stage if we try to use the formulas in column E we would get a circular reference.

As all the references in the formula are fixed with dollar signs, we can just copy the formulas from column E to column G as below:

	A	B	C	D	E	F	G
1	Salesforce	Revenue From Sales	Unique Ref	Order	List with Duplicates Removed	Revenue from Sales	End Ref
2	Adam	£601.00	1	1	Adam	£1,715.00	Adam
3	Bella	£717.00	2	2	Bella	£1,169.00	Bella
4	Charles	£691.00	3	3	Charles	£796.00	Charles
5	Donna	£183.00	4	4	Donna	£714.00	Donna
6	Etnan	£569.00	5	5	Etnan	£1,280.00	Etnan
7	Fiona	£412.00	6	6	Fiona	£909.00	Fiona
8	Michael	£74.00	7	7	Michael	£74.00	Michael
9	Adam	£260.00	7	8	Terry	£657.00	Terry
10	Terry	£657.00	8	9	Katrina	£87.00	Katrina
11	Katrina	£87.00	9	10	Mary	£437.00	Mary
12	Mary	£437.00	10	11			No More Data
13	Adam	£854.00	10	12			No More Data
14	Bella	£452.00	10	13			No More Data
15	Charles	£105.00	10	14			No More Data
16	Donna	£531.00	10	15			No More Data
17	Etnan	£711.00	10	16			No More Data

Then in cell E3 (not E2!) I would amend the existing formula:

=IFERROR(INDEX($A$2:$A$18,MATCH($D3,$C$2:$C$18,0)),"No More Data")

If it is the first time you have used an IFERROR, formula it would be easier to remove the IFERROR before amending the formula.

Looking at column E and column G, I know that when there is no more data my formula returns the words "No More Data" so if a cell says "No More Data" but the cell above does not we know we are at the bottom of the list and one cell under the last of our data. So we would need to add a condition to our formula in cell E3 to say if the cell in column G3 = "No More Data" and the cell above it, G2, does not equal "No More Data" then return "Total". If not, carry on with the formula that you already have:

=IF(AND(G3="No More Data",G2<>"No More Data"),"Total",INDEX($A$2:$A$18,MATCH($D3,"$C$2:$C$18,0)))

I know this looks like a complicated formula but we are just adding a couple of conditions to what we have already built. We have basically just bolted the condition below to the start of it and added a closing bracket at the end.

IF(AND(G3="No More Data",G2<>"No More Data"),"Total",

Once you know the formula is working, we would wrap it with an IFERROR.

IFERROR(IF(AND(G3="No More Data",G2<>"No More Data"),"Total",INDEX($A$2:$A$18,MATCH($D3,$C$2:$C$18,0))),
"No More Data")

Once we copy this down, the results would be as follows:

E	F	G
List with Duplicates Removed	Revenue from Sales	End Ref
Adam	£1,715.00	Adam
Bella	£1,169.00	Bella
Charles	£796.00	Charles
Donna	£714.00	Donna
Etnan	£1,280.00	Etnan
Fiona	£909.00	Fiona
Michael	£74.00	Michael
Terry	£657.00	Terry
Katrina	£87.00	Katrina
Mary	£437.00	Mary
Total		No More Data
		No More Data
		No More Data
		No More Data
		No More Data
		No More Data

We would now need to amend the revenue from sales formula in order to total all of the cells above the row with total on it.

In column F3 (not F2!), we would amend the existing formula:

SUMIFS($B$2:$B$18,$A$2:$A$18,$E3)

We now need to add a condition that says if E3 = "Total", add up whatever is above it. If E3 does not equal "Total", carry on with the formula that you already have.

=if(E2="Total",SUM(F$2:F2), SUMIFS($B$2:$B$18,$A$2:$A$18,$E3))

Please note that the first F2 is a fixed reference so it does not move as we copy the formula down. We always want to add from the first cell with info down to the cell above the total but we want the second F2 to change as we move down to increase our range. So we start with SUM(F$2:F2) and as we copy the formula down we get SUM(F$2:F3), SUM(F$2:F4), SUM(F$2:F5)... and so on.

The results are as follows:

List with Duplicates Removed	Revenue from Sales	End Ref
Adam	£1,715.00	Adam
Bella	£1,169.00	Bella
Charles	£796.00	Charles
Donna	£714.00	Donna
Etnan	£1,280.00	Etnan
Fiona	£909.00	Fiona
Michael	£74.00	Michael
Terry	£657.00	Terry
Katrina	£87.00	Katrina
Mary	£437.00	Mary
Total	£7,838.00	No More Data
		No More Data
		No More Data
		No More Data
		No More Data
		More Data

We now have a dynamic sheet that will remove duplicates and automatically add new salesforce members as they appear, will move the total up or down depending on the change of salesforce members in the data and keep a sum of all the items in the list. Wow!

The last thing I would do to tidy up is apply conditional formatting that says if any row in column E equals "Total" fill it in grey and make the font bold.

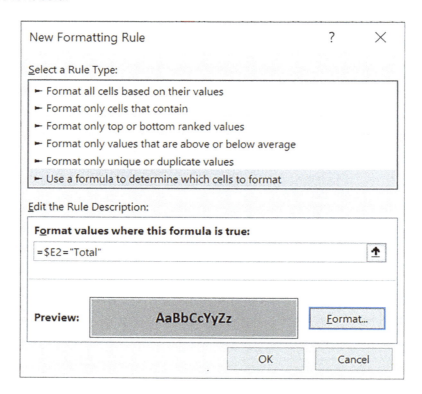

We can now hide columns C, D and G to leave just the data and our dynamic table:

List with Duplicates Removed	Revenue from Sales
Adam	£1,715.00
Bella	£1,169.00
Charles	£796.00
Donna	£714.00
Etnan	£1,280.00
Fiona	£909.00
Michael	£74.00
Terry	£657.00
Katrina	£87.00
Mary	£437.00
Total	£7,838.00

If you now went into your data set and changed Adam in cell A13 to Peter, your table will automatically increase by one and your total would move down from row 12 to row 13 as you have one more salesforce member as below. Peter adds himself in at the bottom and the total shifts down one. The £854 is now removed from Adam and allocated to Peter:

List with Duplicates Removed	Revenue from Sales
Adam	£861.00
Bella	£1,169.00
Charles	£796.00
Donna	£714.00
Etnan	£1,280.00
Fiona	£909.00
Michael	£74.00
Terry	£657.00
Katrina	£87.00
Mary	£437.00
Peter	£854.00
Total	£7,838.00

If we now change Peter back to Adam, and Terry in cell A10 to Adam, our list will reduce by two as we have lost both Peter and Terry but will still give us a neatly wrapped table with a dynamic total at the bottom with no refresh required.

List with Duplicates Removed	Revenue from Sales
Adam	£2,372.00
Bella	£1,169.00
Charles	£796.00
Donna	£714.00
Etnan	£1,280.00
Fiona	£909.00
Michael	£74.00
Katrina	£87.00
Mary	£437.00
Total	£7,838.00

Once you have created this you can either hand it over to your client, without needing to amend it, or having the need to create a macro to update the pivot table any time the data is refreshed as it will update in real time as soon as the data changes.

These examples are quite simple sheets, but you can create sheets that don't just sum in the total, you could have a count total, average total or a percentage total… and they would all work in the same way, you would just amend your condition to produce whatever you needed.

New Data Flags

In some situations where we have new details added to our data, we would not want to automatically incorporate it into our tables. If we have parent and child groupings, we would want to know which group the new details should sit in before including it in our data.

If we had groups of produce, apples and bananas would sit in the child group and the parent group would be fruit or milk, and yoghurt would sit in the child group and the parent group would be dairy. If we had new produce come in that were grapes we would want to ensure we added it to the fruit table not the dairy table.

In order to highlight the new produce so we can decide which group to add it to, we can use a similar technique to the previous chapter.

We would first need the produce that we have listed in a simple table as below:

Child	Parent
Apples	Fruit
Bananas	Fruit
Milk	Dairy
Yoghurt	Dairy
Cheese	Dairy
Pears	Fruit
Oranges	Fruit

Worksheet 1 New Data Flags

In our calculation sheet we would run an INDEX MATCH formula to look in our table and find the produce in the child column. We would wrap this in an IFERROR formula so that it would let us know when the data item was not located in our sheet:

INDEX($A$2:$A$8,MATCH(D2,$A$2:$A$30,0))

Bring in the child name from column A of our table (the Child) where it matches the produce name in our data column D as below.

	A	B	C	D	E	F
1	Child	Parent		Data	Unique Ref	Match
2	Apples	Fruit		Apples	1	=IFERROR(INDEX($A$2:$A$30,MATCH(D2,$A$2:$A$30,0)),"No Match")
3	Bananas	Fruit		Bananas	2	
4	Milk	Dairy		Milk	3	
5	Yoghurt	Dairy		Yoghurt	4	
6	Cheese	Dairy		Cheese	5	
7	Pears	Fruit		Pears	6	
8	Oranges	Fruit		Oranges	7	
9				Grapes	8	

Now we know that if we have any new produce in our data added we will not find a match in our produce table so the formula will return an error. We are best to wrap our formula in an IFERROR to help us identify there were no matching items in our produce table.

IFERROR(INDEX($A$2:$A$30,MATCH(D2,$A$2:$A$30,0))**,"No Match")**

Now if we do not find a match in our produce table, the formula will return "No Match" as we can see below.

	A	B	C	D	E	F	G	H
1	Child	Parent		Data	Unique Ref	Match	Rank1	Rank2
2	Apples	Fruit		Apples	1	Apples		
3	Bananas	Fruit		Bananas	2	Bananas		
4	Milk	Dairy		Milk	3	Milk		
5	Yoghurt	Dairy		Yoghurt	4	Yoghurt		
6	Cheese	Dairy		Cheese	5	Cheese		
7	Pears	Fruit		Pears	6	Pears		
8	Oranges	Fruit		Oranges	7	Oranges		
9				Grapes	8	No Match		
10				Apples	9	Apples		

We now know the position of the new item in our data sheet and can use the Double Rank method to pull the new items into another sheet.

In the Rank1 column we insert a formula to say if our Match column says "No Match" give it a unique reference, if not just put 0 as we are not really interested:

If(F2="No Match",E2,0)

We can see in this example where we have "Grapes", the new produce not in our produce table, the Rank1 column brings in the unique ref on that row:

D	E	F	G	H
Data	Unique Ref	Match	Rank1	Rank2
Apples	1	Apples	0	
Bananas	2	Bananas	0	
Milk	3	Milk	0	
Yoghurt	4	Yoghurt	0	
Cheese	5	Cheese	0	
Pears	6	Pears	0	
Oranges	7	Oranges	0	
Grapes	8	No Match	8	
Apples	9	Apples	0	

As in our previous chapters, the second rank puts the first rank column numbers in a predictable order so we can pick out the items we want. If Rank1 = 0 return 0 as we are not interested in it, if Rank1 is not 0, rank it against the other numbers in the Rank1 column:

IF(G2=0,0,RANK(G2,G2:G30))

	D	E	F	G	H
	Data	Unique Ref	Match	Rank1	Rank2
	Apples	1	Apples	0	0
	Bananas	2	Bananas	0	0
	Milk	3	Milk	0	0
	Yoghurt	4	Yoghurt	0	0
	Cheese	5	Cheese	0	0
	Pears	6	Pears	0	0
	Oranges	7	Oranges	0	0
	Grapes	8	No Match	8	1
	Apples	9	Apples	0	0

We now have a "1" in the Rank2 column on the same row as our new item "Grapes" as this is the first new item we have found. If there were more new items they would be numbered sequentially down the Rank2 column. We can now, as in the Discovery chapter, bring in the new items into a new items table.

Using an INDEX MATCH we can bring in the data where we find the number "1" in Rank 2:

IFERROR(INDEX(D:D,MATCH(E2,H:H,0)),0)

	D	E	F	G	H	I	J
	Data	Unique Ref	Match	Rank1	Rank2		New Items
	Apples	1	Apples	0	0		=INDEX(D:D,MATCH(E2,H:H,0))
	Bananas	2	Bananas	0	0		
	Milk	3	Milk	0	0		
	Yoghurt	4	Yoghurt	0	0		
	Cheese	5	Cheese	0	0		
	Pears	6	Pears	0	0		
	Oranges	7	Oranges	0	0		
	Grapes	8	No Match	8	1		
	Apples	9	Apples	0	0		

	D	E	F	G	H	I	J
	Data	Unique Ref	Match	Rank1	Rank2		New Items
	Apples	1	Apples	0	0		Grapes
	Bananas	2	Bananas	0	0		
	Milk	3	Milk	0	0		
	Yoghurt	4	Yoghurt	0	0		
	Cheese	5	Cheese	0	0		
	Pears	6	Pears	0	0		
	Oranges	7	Oranges	0	0		
	Grapes	8	No Match	8	1		
	Apples	9	Apples	0	0		

The conditional formatting as in the previous chapters would need to be applied in order to hide the blank cells or errors. Once we decide where the new product sits in the produce table we can add it into the table, once we do the new items sheet will go back to being blank (if the conditional formatting has been applied) as there are no longer any items in our data that do not appear in our updated produce list.

Data Dumps – Putting it all Together

Now if you are used to manipulating data you will all be used to the dreaded data dump. This is usually where you have asked for some specific data and you have been sent a massive file with 150+ columns and 10,000 rows and told "it's in there". Some data providers will give you a PDF summary that summarises some of the data but the CSV version is basically a puzzle and the only one that we have a hope of manipulating or drilling down into.

Where I have encountered this in the past and a client or a member of the team need regular reports from that data, or the data is being input in real time by the end user themselves, I bring together all of the techniques that we have discussed to create a bespoke solution that is easy for the client or team to run themselves.

We are going to use the techniques that we have learned so far and put them together to create a template that will automatically sort out your data dump.

In the examples I have previously given, I have put all our formulas next to the data to make it easier to see and explain. In reality, I would create a separate calculation sheet (calcs) where I would put the bulk of my formulas and then hide it so that everything is nice and neat and no one can accidently delete any of the formulas. This also has the added advantage for the client that if there are no formulas on the data sheet they don't have to select large amounts of data and drop them into a specific part of the data sheet in order to not paste over your formulas, they can just dump the whole new page of data into the data sheet.

We will be able to do this because of a neat little trick that Excel can do. When we are using SUMIFS, COUNTIFS or INDEX MATCH functions, as long as they are in alignment, the various sections of the formula can come from completely separate sheets.

What I mean by "in alignment" is if we have a column of INDEX MATCH formulas on our calc sheet that are picking up from our data sheet, the first INDEX MATCH formula must be in the same row as the data it is looking at in the data sheet. If the first name on the data sheet is in row 2, the first formula in the calc sheet needs to be input in row 2 as it is referring to row 2 of the data sheet so that they are aligned. If there is a formula on row 5000 of the data sheet the formula in the calc sheet that is referring to it in the data sheet must be in row 5000 to be aligned.

If we refer back to the New Data Flags chapter we had the data and formulas on the same worksheet, the data in column D and the formulas, Unique Ref, Match, Rank1 and Rank2 were in columns E to H as below.

D	E	F	G	H
Data	Unique Ref	Match	Rank1	Rank2
Apples	1	Apples	0	0
Bananas	2	Bananas	0	0
Milk	3	Milk	0	0
Yoghurt	4	Yoghurt	0	0
Cheese	5	Cheese	0	0
Pears	6	Pears	0	0
Oranges	7	Oranges	0	0
Grapes	8	No Match	8	1
Apples	9	Apples	0	0

We can easily move the calculations in columns E to H into another sheet as long as we ensure the formula in F2 is in row 2 of the calc sheet, G2 is in row 2 of the calc sheet and so on.

The Template

In the data dump worksheet we have 200 rows of data giving a Customer ID, Customer Name, email, New Sales, Commission, Date and Providers.

Obviously you will have your own set of data that you will want to work on but for now use this data to understand the basic system and then you can modify it for your chosen data set. What we are going to create with this is a template that once the data is inserted will dynamically populate:

Clients Page – which will list all of our clients in rank order, summarise their total sales and total commission and give us their percentage split of our total revenue.

Provider Page – which will list all of our providers in rank order, summarise their total sales and total commission and give us their percentage split of our total revenue.

Individual provider pages – which will list all of the clients using that provider in rank order, the total revenue in each month for each client and the total revenue for each month.

The dynamic nature of what we are building means that, once you drop in the new data, if there are any new providers or new clients they will be automatically added and, in turn, if a previous provider or client does not appear in the new data they will not appear on the template. Let's get started!

Below is an example of my data dump with the columns as listed below.

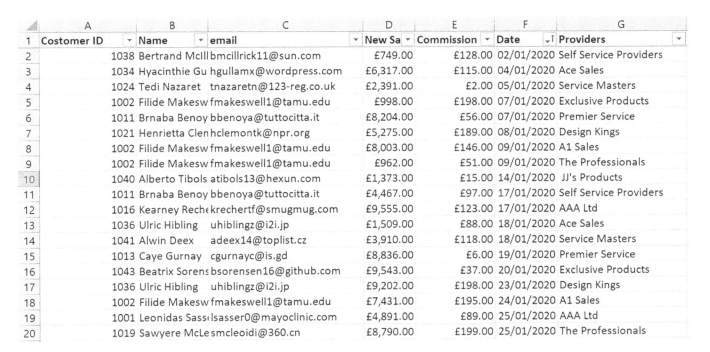

	A	B	C	D	E	F	G
1	Costomer ID	Name	email	New Sa	Commission	Date	Providers
2	1038	Bertrand McIll	bmcillrick11@sun.com	£749.00	£128.00	02/01/2020	Self Service Providers
3	1034	Hyacinthie Gu	hgullamx@wordpress.com	£6,317.00	£115.00	04/01/2020	Ace Sales
4	1024	Tedi Nazaret	tnazaretn@123-reg.co.uk	£2,391.00	£2.00	05/01/2020	Service Masters
5	1002	Filide Makesw	fmakeswell1@tamu.edu	£998.00	£198.00	07/01/2020	Exclusive Products
6	1011	Brnaba Benoy	bbenoya@tuttocitta.it	£8,204.00	£56.00	07/01/2020	Premier Service
7	1021	Henrietta Clen	hclemontk@npr.org	£5,275.00	£189.00	08/01/2020	Design Kings
8	1002	Filide Makesw	fmakeswell1@tamu.edu	£8,003.00	£146.00	09/01/2020	A1 Sales
9	1002	Filide Makesw	fmakeswell1@tamu.edu	£962.00	£51.00	09/01/2020	The Professionals
10	1040	Alberto Tibols	atibols13@hexun.com	£1,373.00	£15.00	14/01/2020	JJ's Products
11	1011	Brnaba Benoy	bbenoya@tuttocitta.it	£4,467.00	£97.00	17/01/2020	Self Service Providers
12	1016	Kearney Reche	krechertf@smugmug.com	£9,555.00	£123.00	17/01/2020	AAA Ltd
13	1036	Ulric Hibling	uhiblingz@i2i.jp	£1,509.00	£88.00	18/01/2020	Ace Sales
14	1041	Alwin Deex	adeex14@toplist.cz	£3,910.00	£118.00	18/01/2020	Service Masters
15	1013	Caye Gurnay	cgurnayc@is.gd	£8,836.00	£6.00	19/01/2020	Premier Service
16	1043	Beatrix Sorens	bsorensen16@github.com	£9,543.00	£37.00	20/01/2020	Exclusive Products
17	1036	Ulric Hibling	uhiblingz@i2i.jp	£9,202.00	£198.00	23/01/2020	Design Kings
18	1002	Filide Makesw	fmakeswell1@tamu.edu	£7,431.00	£195.00	24/01/2020	A1 Sales
19	1001	Leonidas Sass	lsasser0@mayoclinic.com	£4,891.00	£89.00	25/01/2020	AAA Ltd
20	1019	Sawyere McLe	smcleoidi@360.cn	£8,790.00	£199.00	25/01/2020	The Professionals

Data Dump Data Sheet

Clients Page

The first thing we need to do is create a new worksheet for our calculations (calcs). In column A we are going to put our reference which will be the same as we did in the Discovery chapter, just sequential numbers from one to as many as you need. This will need to run to at least the number of rows you have on the Data Sheet plus some extra so you have room for the data to grow. On this example we have 200 rows of data for the entire year so if we took my references and formulas to row 500 it would give us a good cushion for expansion.

In order for the references and formulas in the Calcs sheet to be aligned with the data in the Data Sheet, the first reference needs to be in cell A2 as A1 on the Calcs sheet holds the column heading, the first cell with data that we need is cell A2. So in column A2 of the Calcs sheet we put number one in A3 we put number two and so on down to number 500 in cell A501.

In column B we need to apply the formula to remove duplicates from our client list so each client only appears once as we did in the Dynamic Sheets chapter. The difference being that we are now looking at data on a separate sheet (Data Sheet) with the formula being written in the Calcs sheet.

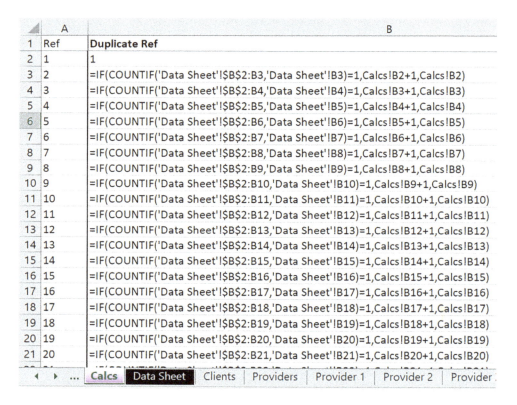

IF(COUNTIF('Data Sheet'!$B$2:B3,'Data Sheet'!B3)=1,Calcs!B2+1,Calcs!B2)

This formula is looking at the Data Sheet and saying count how many times the name in the Data Sheet B3 appears from B2 to B3. If it only appears once (so the count =1) then add one to the number in the previous cell (so it creates a new number, a unique reference) if it does not equal one, meaning the name has appeared before, use the same number as in the previous cell. So as we move down the Duplicate Ref column any time there is a new name the number would increase by one and any time there is a duplicate the number would stay the same. This means that any time there is a new number in the Duplicate Ref column of the Calcs sheet there is a corresponding new name in the same row of the Duplicate Ref column on the Data Sheet.

Above us on the left we have the Calcs sheet and on the right we have the Data Sheet. We can see that the client Filde Makeswell appears multiple times, the first time she appears is on row 5 so it generates a new number one greater than on the previous column on the Calcs sheet. When the name appears again on rows 8 and 9 as this is not the first time that the name has appeared it does not generate a new unique reference and repeats the number that we had before.

This means that when we run our LOOKUP/INDEX MATCH we can select unique names only and will have no duplicates in our list. Once you have the formula working I would wrap it in an IFERROR that would return the previous number if an error was found.

IFERROR(IF(COUNTIF('Data Sheet'!$B$2:B3,'Data Sheet'!B3)=1,Calcs!B2+1,Calcs!B2),Calcs!B2)

In column C of the Calcs sheet create a title of "Client – Duplicates Removed" so we can create a LOOKUP to bring in our unique names as we did in the Dynamic Sheets chapter.

We need to bring in the client names from the Data Sheet where it matches our ref on the Calcs sheet. So we would match the number 1 in our ref column (our first unique name) with number 1 in the Duplicate Ref column. As the formula moved down we would match number 2 (our second unique name) with the number 2 in our Duplicate Ref column and so on.

INDEX('Data Sheet'!$B:$B,MATCH(Calcs!$A2,Calcs!$B:$B,0))

	A	B
1	Costomer ID ▾	Name
2	1038	Bertrand McIllrick
3	1034	Hyacinthie Gullam
4	1024	Tedi Nazaret
5	1002	Filide Makeswell
6	1011	Brnaba Benoy
7	1021	Henrietta Clemont
8	1002	Filide Makeswell
9	1002	Filide Makeswell
10	1040	Alberto Tibols
11	1011	Brnaba Benoy
12	1016	Kearney Rechert
13	1036	Ulric Hibling
14	1041	Alwin Deex
15	1013	Caye Gurnay
16	1043	Beatrix Sorensen
17	1036	Ulric Hibling
18	1002	Filide Makeswell
19	1001	Leonidas Sasser
20	1019	Sawyere McLeoid
21	1038	Bertrand McIllrick

Tabs: ◀ ▶ … | Calcs | **Data Sheet** | Clients

	A	B	C
1		Duplicate Ref	Client - Duplicates Removed
2	1		1 Bertrand McIllrick
3	2		2 Hyacinthie Gullam
4	3		3 Tedi Nazaret
5	4		4 Filide Makeswell
6	5		5 Brnaba Benoy
7	6		6 Henrietta Clemont
8	7		6 Alberto Tibols
9	8		6 Kearney Rechert
10	9		7 Ulric Hibling
11	10		7 Alwin Deex
12	11		8 Caye Gurnay
13	12		9 Beatrix Sorensen
14	13		10 Leonidas Sasser
15	14		11 Sawyere McLeoid
16	15		12 Nessa Kettel
17	16		12 Skye Tittershill
18	17		12 Otis Stollery
19	18		13 Kevan Henkens
20	19		14 Heidie Leathlay
21	20		14 May Foat

Tabs: ◀ ▶ … | Calcs | **Data Sheet** | Clients | Providers

On the left we have the Data Sheet and on the right we have the Calcs sheet. We can see on the right that the names are brought in in order and when it finds a duplicate it skips to the next unique name. After Henrietta Clemont on the left, Filde Makeswell appears again, so on the right it skips to the next unique name which is Alberto Tibols.

Once you have your formula working, I would wrap it in an IFERROR that would return a zero in the event of an error.

IFERROR(INDEX('Data Sheet'!$B:$B,MATCH(Calcs!$A2,Calcs!$B:$B,0))**,0)**

We now have our list of clients with the duplicates removed.

We now need a simple formula to total the revenue earned by each client so we can rank them. Create a "Client Revenue" column in column D of the Calcs sheet. As this is made up of two figures, the "New Sales" and the "Commission", we will need to create two formulas and add them together (please see the Toolkit for info on SUMIFS).

So we need to add all the "New Sales" for the clients which are in column D of the Data Sheet where the name in column B of the Data Sheet matches our client name on the Calcs sheet:

SUMIFS('Data Sheet'!D:D,'Data Sheet'!B:B,Calcs!C2)

Add all the amounts in column D of the Data Sheet where column B matches our client name.

And we need to add all the Commission for the clients which are in column E of the Data Sheet where the name in column B of the Data Sheet matches our client name on the Calcs sheet:

SUMIFS('Data Sheet'!E:E,'Data Sheet'!B:B,Calcs!C2)

Add all the amounts in column E of the Data Sheet where column B matches our client name.

We simply add the two formulas together with a plus sign. When we join the formulas together, they would look like this:

SUMIFS('Data Sheet'!D:D,'Data Sheet'!B:B,Calcs!C2)+SUMIFS('Data Sheet'!E:E,'Data Sheet'!B:B,Calcs!C2)

	A	B	C	D
1		Duplicate Ref	Client - Duplicates Removed	Client Revenue
2	1		1 Bertrand McIllrick	£19,225.00
3	2		2 Hyacinthie Gullam	£16,567.00
4	3		3 Tedi Nazaret	£22,027.00
5	4		4 Filide Makeswell	£18,997.00
6	5		5 Brnaba Benoy	£27,062.00
7	6		6 Henrietta Clemont	£25,013.00
8	7		6 Alberto Tibols	£25,524.00
9	8		6 Kearney Rechert	£17,539.00
10	9		7 Ulric Hibling	£16,256.00
11	10		7 Alwin Deex	£14,360.00
12	11		8 Caye Gurnay	£28,221.00
13	12		9 Beatrix Sorensen	£21,935.00
14	13		10 Leonidas Sasser	£30,763.00
15	14		11 Sawyere McLeoid	£30,629.00
16	15		12 Nessa Kettel	£24,552.00
17	16		12 Skye Tittershill	£10,083.00
18	17		12 Otis Stollery	£28,637.00
19	18		13 Kevan Henkens	£15,064.00
20	19		14 Heidie Leathlay	£26,208.00
21	20		14 May Foat	£15,807.00

... | Calcs | Data Sheet | Clients | Providers | Provider 1

Where there is no client name the SUM formula will return a zero.

We now just need to rank the Client Revenue from largest to smallest and we have our data for the Clients page.

As where there is no client name we will have a zero, we do not want this to appear in our rank as there will be no client information to display so to avoid this we need to add a condition, or "IF", to our rank formula.

In column E of our Calcs sheet we would create a "Client Rank" heading. The simple RANK formula would be to rank the clients' revenue in relation to the other clients' revenue. To add the condition, or "IF", we need to say if the amount in column D = 0, put a zero and don't bother to rank it, if it is not a zero, rank it as per the formula (IF D2=0 put 0).

IF(D2=0,0,RANK(D2,$D$2:$D$201))

We would need to add a tie breaker (see the Toolkit) to ensure that each client had a separate rank even if their revenue was the same (no ties allowed):

IF(D2=0,0,RANK(D2,$D$2:$D$201)+COUNTIF($D$2:D2,D2)-1)

The tie breaker basically says if it finds the same rank above it in the list, make the result of the count one less.

IF(D2=0,0,RANK(D2,$D$2:$D$201)+COUNTIF($D$2:D2,D2)-1)

	A	B	C	D	E
1		Duplicate Ref	Client - Duplicates Removed	Client Revenue	Client Rank
2	1	1 Bertrand McIllrick		£19,225.00	25
3	2	2 Hyacinthie Gullam		£16,567.00	32
4	3	3 Tedi Nazaret		£22,027.00	18
5	4	4 Filide Makeswell		£18,997.00	26
6	5	5 Brnaba Benoy		£27,062.00	7
7	6	6 Henrietta Clemont		£25,013.00	10
8	7	6 Alberto Tibols		£25,524.00	9
9	8	6 Kearney Rechert		£17,539.00	30
10	9	7 Ulric Hibling		£16,256.00	36
11	10	7 Alwin Deex		£14,360.00	41
12	11	8 Caye Gurnay		£28,221.00	6
13	12	9 Beatrix Sorensen		£21,935.00	19
14	13	10 Leonidas Sasser		£30,763.00	2
15	14	11 Sawyere McLeoid		£30,629.00	3
16	15	12 Nessa Kettel		£24,552.00	11
17	16	12 Skye Tittershill		£10,083.00	46
18	17	12 Otis Stollery		£28,637.00	5
19	18	13 Kevan Henkens		£15,064.00	39
20	19	14 Heidie Leathlay		£26,208.00	8
21	20	14 May Foat		£15,807.00	38

◀ ▶ ... | Calcs | Data Sheet | Clients | Providers | Provider 1 | Provider 2

We now have a list of clients with the duplicates removed, their total revenue and their rank by revenue. We can now create the dynamic "Clients" page.

Create a new page and call it "Clients".

For the Clients page we simply start with the headers:

Client	New Sales	Commission	Total	%

We are first going to bring in the client names in rank order, as we have already done the work on the Calcs sheet all we need to do is create an INDEX MATCH to bring in the names we have in column C of the Calcs sheet (which have already had the duplicates removed) where the rank number matches in column E on the Calc sheet (Client Rank). As we already have the numbers 1 to 200 in column A of the Calcs sheet, we can use this as the rank number that we are matching to:

INDEX(Calcs!$C:$C,MATCH(Calcs!$A2,Calcs!$E:$E,0))

So, we are bringing in the "Client – Duplicate Removed" from the Calcs sheet where we match the number in A2 of the Calcs sheet, "Ref" (the number one), in column E of the Calcs sheet, "Client Rank". This is the same principal that we used in the Dynamic Sheets chapter.

For the "New Sales" column all we need to do is add up all of the new sales for the client from column D of the Data Sheet where the client name matches our client names in our "Client" column that we have just created. We simply use a SUMIFS formula as before:

SUMIFS('Data Sheet'!$D:$D,'Data Sheet'!$B:$B,Clients!$A2)

Add up all of the "New Sales" in column D of the Data Sheet where the client name appears in column B of the Data Sheet.

We do the same with the "Commission" column, the only difference being that we add the numbers in the Commission column E instead of column D:

SUMIFS('Data Sheet'!$E:$E,'Data Sheet'!$B:$B,Clients!$A2)

The "Total" column count would be the "New Sales" figure and the "Commission" figure added together:

SUM(B2:C2)

We will come back to the percentage column later, our Client sheet should look like this:

	A	B	C	D	E
1	Client	New Sales	Commission	Total	%
2	Fallon McDonnell	£33,684.00	£510.00	£34,194.00	

We can now copy our formulas down the page to bring in the lower ranked clients. As we know from the Calcs sheet, there are only 50 unique clients in the data, in order to leave room for expansion we will copy the formulas down to line 100, on your own projects you may wish to make your sheets larger depending on your needs.

Again, as we did in the Dynamic Sheets chapter, we can wrap the sheet in a border and add a total at the end of the data. The "Total" formula would start in column A3 of the Client sheet and look like this:

IF(AND(Calcs!C3=0,Calcs!C2<>0),"Total",INDEX(Calcs!$C:$C,MATCH(Calcs!$A3,Calcs!$E:$E,0))**)**

We have simply added the condition at the front to say when we reach the end of our list of clients insert the word "Total" and added a bracket to the end of the formula to balance out the IF.

In the New Sales and Commission columns we need to add the formula to add everything in the column above where we find the word "Total" on that row:

New Sales (Column B of the Clients sheet)

IF(A3="Total",SUM(B$2:B2),SUMIFS('Data Sheet'!$D:$D,'Data Sheet'!$B:$B,Clients!$A3))

So if the Clients column says "Total", add all the numbers above the current cell in this column, if not, continue with the SUMIF formula we already had in place. As the SUM formula moves down the column the range we are adding will expand from B$2:B3 to B$2:B4 and so on until we reach the bottom of our range, but never including the row we are on as this would create a circular reference.

A	B
Clients	**New Sales**
Fallon McDonnell	=SUMIFS('Data Sheet'!$D:$D,'Data Sheet'!$B:$B,Clients!$A2)
Filide Makeswell	=IF(A3="Total",SUM($B$2:B2),SUMIFS('Data Sheet'!$D:$D,'Data Sheet'!$B:$B,Clients!$A3))
Brnaba Benoy	=IF(A4="Total",SUM($B$2:B3),SUMIFS('Data Sheet'!$D:$D,'Data Sheet'!$B:$B,Clients!$A4))
Ulric Hibling	=IF(A5="Total",SUM($B$2:B4),SUMIFS('Data Sheet'!$D:$D,'Data Sheet'!$B:$B,Clients!$A5))
Nessa Kettel	=IF(A6="Total",SUM($B$2:B5),SUMIFS('Data Sheet'!$D:$D,'Data Sheet'!$B:$B,Clients!$A6))
Kearney Rechert	=IF(A7="Total",SUM($B$2:B6),SUMIFS('Data Sheet'!$D:$D,'Data Sheet'!$B:$B,Clients!$A7))
Beatrix Sorensen	=IF(A8="Total",SUM($B$2:B7),SUMIFS('Data Sheet'!$D:$D,'Data Sheet'!$B:$B,Clients!$A8))
Caye Gurnay	=IF(A9="Total",SUM($B$2:B8),SUMIFS('Data Sheet'!$D:$D,'Data Sheet'!$B:$B,Clients!$A9))
Libbi Ferronel	=IF(A10="Total",SUM($B$2:B9),SUMIFS('Data Sheet'!$D:$D,'Data Sheet'!$B:$B,Clients!$A10))
Lonee Beatey	=IF(A11="Total",SUM($B$2:B10),SUMIFS('Data Sheet'!$D:$D,'Data Sheet'!$B:$B,Clients!$A11))
Sylas McNirlin	=IF(A12="Total",SUM($B$2:B11),SUMIFS('Data Sheet'!$D:$D,'Data Sheet'!$B:$B,Clients!$A12))
Hyacinthie Gullam	=IF(A13="Total",SUM($B$2:B12),SUMIFS('Data Sheet'!$D:$D,'Data Sheet'!$B:$B,Clients!$A13))
Hattie Spatig	=IF(A14="Total",SUM($B$2:B13),SUMIFS('Data Sheet'!$D:$D,'Data Sheet'!$B:$B,Clients!$A14))
Henrietta Clemont	=IF(A15="Total",SUM($B$2:B14),SUMIFS('Data Sheet'!$D:$D,'Data Sheet'!$B:$B,Clients!$A15))
Alwin Deex	=IF(A16="Total",SUM($B$2:B15),SUMIFS('Data Sheet'!$D:$D,'Data Sheet'!$B:$B,Clients!$A16))
Alecia Cattle	=IF(A17="Total",SUM($B$2:B16),SUMIFS('Data Sheet'!$D:$D,'Data Sheet'!$B:$B,Clients!$A17))
May Foat	=IF(A18="Total",SUM($B$2:B17),SUMIFS('Data Sheet'!$D:$D,'Data Sheet'!$B:$B,Clients!$A18))
Tedi Nazaret	=IF(A19="Total",SUM($B$2:B18),SUMIFS('Data Sheet'!$D:$D,'Data Sheet'!$B:$B,Clients!$A19))
Georgena Trask	=IF(A20="Total",SUM($B$2:B19),SUMIFS('Data Sheet'!$D:$D,'Data Sheet'!$B:$B,Clients!$A20))
Alberto Tibols	=IF(A21="Total",SUM($B$2:B20),SUMIFS('Data Sheet'!$D:$D,'Data Sheet'!$B:$B,Clients!$A21))
Bertrand McIllrick	=IF(A22="Total",SUM($B$2:B21),SUMIFS('Data Sheet'!$D:$D,'Data Sheet'!$B:$B,Clients!$A22))
Total	**=IF(A23="Total",SUM($B$2:B22),SUMIFS('Data Sheet'!$D:$D,'Data Sheet'!$B:$B,Clients!$A23))**

This means that once we have listed all of the client names, after we have automatically removed the duplicates, the formula will insert the word "Total" in column A. Once the formulas in column B detect the word "Total" it will add all the numbers above it in column B giving us the total new sales for all of our clients. As this is dynamic, if a client is removed from the data sheet the total would move up a row and if a client is added it would move down a row.

Clients	New Sales
Fallon McDonnell	£33,684.00
Filide Makeswell	£17,394.00
Brnaba Benoy	£14,661.00
Ulric Hibling	£10,711.00
Nessa Kettel	£9,847.00
Kearney Rechert	£9,555.00
Beatrix Sorensen	£9,543.00
Caye Gurnay	£8,836.00
Libbi Ferronel	£8,370.00
Lonee Beatey	£7,660.00
Sylas McNirlin	£6,758.00
Hyacinthie Gullam	£6,317.00
Hattie Spatig	£5,928.00
Henrietta Clemont	£5,275.00
Alwin Deex	£3,910.00
Alecia Cattle	£3,723.00
May Foat	£2,451.00
Tedi Nazaret	£2,391.00
Georgena Trask	£1,997.00
Alberto Tibols	£1,373.00
Bertrand McIllrick	£749.00
Total	£171,133.00

Apply conditional formatting as we did in the Dynamic Sheets chapter "IF A2= "Total" fill it in grey and make the font bold.

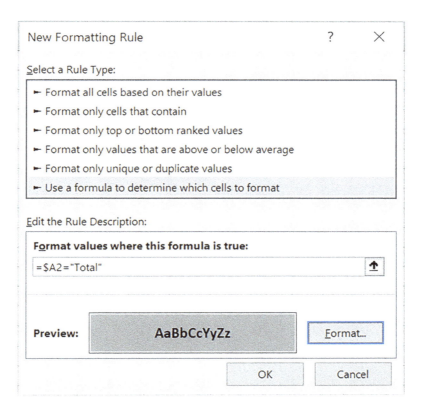

For "Commission" we would repeat the process we just did for column B, "New Sales", in column C, "Commission", adding only the section in red as below and adding a closing bracket at the end to balance the IF.

Commission

IF(A3="Total",SUM($C$2:C2),SUMIFS('Data Sheet'!$E:$E,'Data Sheet'!$B:$B,Clients!$A3))

To complete the Client sheet we can add a formula in the Total column that simply adds the "New Sales" and the "Commission" together:

=SUM(B2:C2)

And in the "%" column we just need to divide the total for each client by the overall total. For this, as we don't know where the total will be due to the dynamic nature of the table, I would use an INDEX MATCH formula to find the overall total:

D2/INDEX(D:D,MATCH("Total",A:A,0))

Divide the Client total (D2) by the result of the INDEX MATCH.

Bring in the number in column D where you find "Total" in column A

Provider Page

We need to go back to the Calcs sheet and in column F follow the same process to remove the duplicates as we did for the Client sheet, we will call this column "Providers". The only difference being that we will look in column G where the provider name is, not column B where the Client name was. So in column F of the Calcs sheet we would put a one in cell F2 and the below in cell F3:

IF(COUNTIF('Data Sheet'!$G$2:G3,'Data Sheet'!G3)=1,Calcs!F2+1,Calcs!F2)

As before, copy these formulas down to row 501 in line with the other calculations and once we are happy it works, wrap it in an "IFERROR" as before.

We now need to repeat the process we did for the clients for the providers. Label columns G, H and I as below:

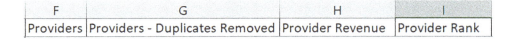

F	G	H	I
Providers	Providers - Duplicates Removed	Provider Revenue	Provider Rank

We can now repeat the formulas in columns C, D and E in columns G, H and I respectively with the only changes being that we are referring to providers now instead of clients (formulas in column C, "Clients – Duplicates Removed", repeated in column G, "Providers - Duplicates Removed", formulas in column D, "Client Revenue", repeated in column H, "Provider Revenue", and the formula in column E, "Client Rank", repeated in column I, "Provider Rank":

Column C changes

From:

=IFERROR(INDEX('Data Sheet'!$B:$B,MATCH(Calcs!$A2,Calcs!$B:$B,0)),0)

To:

=IFERROR(INDEX('Data Sheet'!$G:$G,MATCH(Calcs!$A2,Calcs!$F:$F,0)),0)

Data Sheet column B held the "Client" name so we changed to column G which is the "Provider" name.

And Calcs column B was our "Duplicates Removed" reference numbers for the clients, so we change this to Calcs column F for our "Providers - Duplicates Removed".

Column D changes

From:

=SUMIFS('Data Sheet'!$D:$D,'Data Sheet'!$B:$B,Calcs!C2)+SUMIFS('Data Sheet'!$E:$E,'Data Sheet'!$B:$B,Calcs!C2)

To:

=SUMIFS('Data Sheet'!$D:$D,'Data Sheet'!$G:$G,Calcs!G2)+SUMIFS('Data Sheet'!$E:$E,'Data Sheet'!$G:$G,Calcs!G2)

Data Sheet column B held the "Client" name so we changed to column G which is the "Provider" name.

And Calcs column C was our list of clients with duplicates removed so we change this to Calcs column G, our list of providers with duplicates removed.

Column E changes

From:

=IF(D2=0,0,RANK(D2,$D$2:$D$201)+COUNTIF($D$2:D2,D2)-1)

To:

=IF(H2=0,0,RANK(H2,$H$2:$H$21)+COUNTIF($H$2:H2,H2)-1)

Column D referred to the "Client Revenue" so we changed it to column H which is the "Provider Revenue".

And Calcs column C was our list of clients with duplicates removed, so we change this to Cals column G, our list of providers with duplicates removed.

If this all seems a bit complex we can just create new formulas that will pick up the "Provider" details instead of the "Client" details.

F	G	H	I
Providers	Providers - Duplicates Removed	Provider Revenue	Provider Rank
1	Self Service Providers	£90,690.00	7
2	Ace Sales	£90,690.00	8
3	Service Masters	£115,475.00	2
4	Exclusive Products	£97,910.00	5
5	Premier Service	£105,037.00	3
6	Design Kings	£72,186.00	10
7	A1 Sales	£83,326.00	9
8	The Professionals	£94,858.00	6
9	JJ's Products	£102,280.00	4
9	AAA Ltd	£117,010.00	1
10	0	£0.00	0
10	0	£0.00	0

We now need to create the "Provider" page which will be a replica of the "Clients" page with a few minor changes. We would set up the sheet as below as in the Clients sheet we leave cell A1 blank:

A	B	C	D	E
	New Sales	Commission	Total	%

In Ccell A2 we use the same formula as cell A2 in the Clients sheet but with the following changes.

From:

=IFERROR(INDEX(Calcs!$C:$C,MATCH(Calcs!$A2,Calcs!$E:$E,0)),0)

To:

=IFERROR(INDEX(Calcs!$G:$G,MATCH(Calcs!$A2,Calcs!$I:$I,0)),0)

Calcs $C:$C referred to the Calcs sheet "Client - Duplicates Removed" column so we change this to Calcs $G:$G to now refer to the Calcs sheet "Providers – Duplicates Removed" column.

Calcs $E:$E referred to the Calcs sheet "Client Rank" column so we change this to Calcs $I:$I to now refer to the Calcs sheet "Provider Rank" column.

	A	B	C	D	E
1		New Sales	Commission	Total	%
2	IFERROR(INDEX(Calcs!$G:$G,MATCH(Calcs!$A2,Calcs!$I:$I,0)),0)				

Cell B2 will be the same as B2 in the Clients sheet with the following change.

From:

=SUMIFS('Data Sheet'!$D:$D,'Data Sheet'!$B:$B,Clients!$A2)

To:

=SUMIFS('Data Sheet'!$D:$D,'Data Sheet'!$G:$G,Providers!$A2)

Data Sheet $B:$B refers to the client name so we change this to Data Sheet $G:$G the provider name.

Clients!$A2 refers to A2 on the Clients page so we change this to Providers!$A2 which is A2 on the Provider sheet.

	A	B
1		New Sales
2	AAA Ltd	=SUMIFS('Data Sheet'!D:D,'Data Sheet'!$G:$G,Providers!$A2)

	A	B
1		**New Sales**
2	**AAA Ltd**	£114,854.00

Cell C2 will be the same as C2 in the Clients sheet with the following change.

From:

=SUMIFS('Data Sheet'!$E:$E,'Data Sheet'**!$B:$B,Clients!$A2**)

To:

=SUMIFS('Data Sheet'!E:E,'Data Sheet'**!$G:$G,Providers!$A2**)

Data Sheet **$B:$B** refers to the client name so we change this to Data Sheet **$G:$G** the provider name.

Clients!$A2 refers to A2 on the Clients page so we change this to **Providers!$A2** which is A2 on the Provider sheet.

The "Total" and "%" formulas in cells D2 and E2 will be exactly the same as in the Clients sheet but referring to the Provider sheet.

We can now repeat the process for adding in the "Total" formula in column A and applying the conditional formatting as we did on the Clients sheet.

We can now copy our formulas down the page to bring in the lower ranked clients. As we know from the Calcs sheet, there are only 10 unique providers in the data but in order to leave room for expansion we will copy the formulas down to line 100 to match the client list. On your own projects you may wish to make your sheets larger depending on your needs.

Again, as we did in the Dynamic Sheets chapter, we can wrap the sheet in a border and add a "Total" at the end of the data. The Total formula would start in column A3 of the Provider sheet and look like this:

IF(AND(Calcs!G3=0,Calcs!G2<>0),"Total",INDEX(Calcs!$G:$G,MATCH(Calcs!$F3,Calcs!$I:$I,0))**)**

We have simply added the condition at the front to say when we reach the end of our list of providers insert the word "Total" and added a bracket to the end of the formula to balance out the IF.

In the "New Sales" and "Commission" columns we need to add the formula to add everything in the column above where we find the word "Total" on that row:

New Sales

IF(A3="Total",SUM(B$2:B2),**SUMIFS('Data Sheet'!$D:$D,'Data Sheet'!$B:$B,Providers!$A3))**

So if the Provider column says "Total" add all the numbers above the current cell in this column, if not continue with the SUMIF formula we already had in place. As the SUM formula moves down the column the range we are adding will expand from B$2:B3 to B$2:B4 and so on until we reach the bottom of our range, but never including the row we are on as this would create a circular reference.

	A	B
1		**New Sales**
2	AAA Ltd	=SUMIFS('Data Sheet'!D:D,'Data Sheet'!$G:$G,Providers!$A2)
3	Service Masters	=IF(A3="Total",SUM($B$2:B2),SUMIFS('Data Sheet'!D:D,'Data Sheet'!$G:$G,Providers!$A3))
4	Premier Service	=IF(A4="Total",SUM($B$2:B3),SUMIFS('Data Sheet'!D:D,'Data Sheet'!$G:$G,Providers!$A4))
5	JJ's Products	=IF(A5="Total",SUM($B$2:B4),SUMIFS('Data Sheet'!D:D,'Data Sheet'!$G:$G,Providers!$A5))
6	Exclusive Products	=IF(A6="Total",SUM($B$2:B5),SUMIFS('Data Sheet'!D:D,'Data Sheet'!$G:$G,Providers!$A6))
7	The Professionals	=IF(A7="Total",SUM($B$2:B6),SUMIFS('Data Sheet'!D:D,'Data Sheet'!$G:$G,Providers!$A7))
8	Self Service Providers	=IF(A8="Total",SUM($B$2:B7),SUMIFS('Data Sheet'!D:D,'Data Sheet'!$G:$G,Providers!$A8))
9	Ace Sales	=IF(A9="Total",SUM($B$2:B8),SUMIFS('Data Sheet'!D:D,'Data Sheet'!$G:$G,Providers!$A9))
10	A1 Sales	=IF(A10="Total",SUM($B$2:B9),SUMIFS('Data Sheet'!D:D,'Data Sheet'!$G:$G,Providers!$A10))
11	Design Kings	=IF(A11="Total",SUM($B$2:B10),SUMIFS('Data Sheet'!D:D,'Data Sheet'!$G:$G,Providers!$A11))

This means that once we have listed all of the client names, after we have automatically removed the duplicates, the formula will insert the word "Total" in column A. Once the formulas in column B detect the word "Total" it will add all the numbers above it in column B giving us the total new sales for all of our clients. As this is dynamic, if a client is removed from the data sheet the total would move up a row and if a client is added it would move down a row.

	A	B	C	D	E
1		**New Sales**	**Commission**	**Total**	**%**
2	AAA Ltd	£114,854.00	£2,156.00	£117,010.00	12.07%
3	Service Masters	£113,518.00	£1,957.00	£115,475.00	11.91%
4	Premier Service	£103,378.00	£1,659.00	£105,037.00	10.83%
5	JJ's Products	£100,263.00	£2,017.00	£102,280.00	10.55%
6	Exclusive Products	£96,017.00	£1,893.00	£97,910.00	10.10%
7	The Professionals	£92,557.00	£2,301.00	£94,858.00	9.78%
8	Self Service Providers	£88,366.00	£2,324.00	£90,690.00	9.35%
9	Ace Sales	£88,961.00	£1,729.00	£90,690.00	9.35%
10	A1 Sales	£80,960.00	£2,366.00	£83,326.00	8.60%
11	Design Kings	£69,844.00	£2,342.00	£72,186.00	7.45%
12	Total	£948,718.00	£20,744.00	£969,462.00	100.00%

Apply conditional formatting as we did in the Dynamic Sheets chapter "IF A2= "Total" fill it in grey and make the font bold.

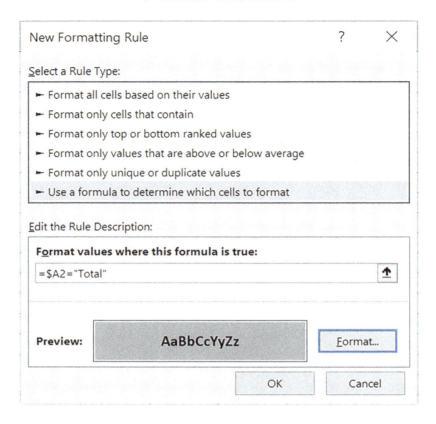

For "Commission", we would do the same thing in column C adding only the section in red as below and adding a closing bracket at the end.

Commission

IF(A3="Total",SUM($C$2:C2),**SUMIFS('Data Sheet'!$E:$E,'Data Sheet'!$B:$B,Providers!$A3))**

To complete the Provider sheet we can add a formula in the Total column that simply adds the "New Sales" and the "Commission" together:

=SUM(B2:C2)

And in the "%" column we just need to divide the total for each client by the overall total. For this I would use an INDEX MATCH formula to find the overall total:

D2/INDEX(D:D,MATCH("Total",A:A,0))

Divide the Client total (D2) by the result of the index match.

Bring in the number in column D where you find "Total" in column A.

We now have a fully dynamic Client and Provider page so if any clients or providers are added to or removed from the data or to the data they will be automatically added or removed from your pages and the totals will recalculate automatically as we have all the formulas in place. But we are not going to stop there, strap in!

Provider Client Details

It would be very useful from this set of data to see when or how often we are paid by a provider or client so let's build something to do that for us.

In our Calcs sheet we have used up to column I. What we will do next is bring in the provider with the highest revenue. We already have this listed in column I, the "Provider Rank" column, so we simply need to create a LOOKUP to pick up the number one ranked provider from our list. In cell J1 we need to input the following formula:

INDEX($G$2:$G$11,MATCH($A$2,$I$2:$I$11,0))

Bring in the provider in column G where column I matches A2 on the Calcs sheet, A2 was our number series that ran from one to 200, A2 being "1". As we can see below, the provider with the number one rank is "AAA Ltd".

F	G	H	I	J
Providers	Providers - Duplicates Removed	Provider Revenue	Provider Rank	=INDEX($G$2:$G$11,MATCH($A$2,$I$2:$I$11,0))
1	Self Service Providers	£90,690.00	7	
2	Ace Sales	£90,690.00	8	
3	Service Masters	£115,475.00	2	
4	Exclusive Products	£97,910.00	5	
5	Premier Service	£105,037.00	3	
6	Design Kings	£72,186.00	10	
7	A1 Sales	£83,326.00	9	
8	The Professionals	£94,858.00	6	
9	JJ's Products	£102,280.00	4	
9	AAA Ltd	£117,010.00	1	
10	0	£0.00	0	

We are now going to use the Double Rank technique in cell J2 to generate a number anytime it finds "AAA Ltd" in the provider column (Column G) of the Data Sheet:

IF('Data Sheet'!$G2=Calcs!J$1,Calcs!$A2,0)

If the provider in cell G2 of the data sheet is "AAA Ltd" bring in the number in the same row from column A of the Calcs sheet, if it does not equal "AAA Ltd" insert a zero. Now copy the formula down the page in column J.

This means wherever the formula brings in a number into column J of the Calcs sheet the provider name "AAA Ltd" will be on the exact same row in the data sheet:

As we can see from below (for ease I have added the Data Sheet and the Calcs sheet side by side in the below diagram), "AAA Ltd" first appears on row 12 of the Data Sheet so the first number is inserted into the Calcs sheet on row 12. In column J of the Calcs sheet, where we locate "AAA Ltd" in column G of the Data Sheet, we pull in the ref on the same row.

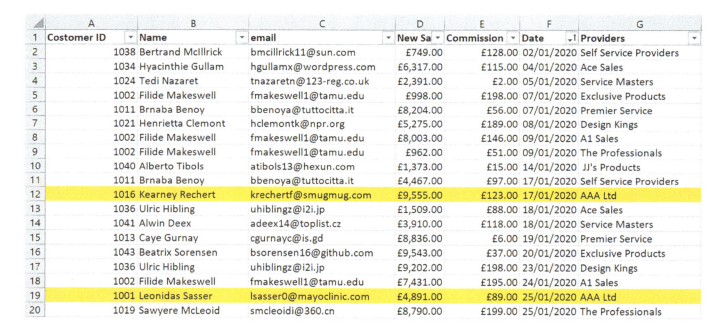

We can now create our RANK formula in column K of the Calcs sheet to put our numbers in column J into a predictable order:

IF(J2=0,0,RANK(J2,J$2:J$201)) (only use dollar signs where I have used dollar signs as this will help us later on).

If J2 = 0, meaning "AAA Ltd" does not appear in that row of the Data Sheet put a zero. If not, and therefore there is a number, rank it against the other numbers in that column.

	J	K
1	AAA Ltd	Rank
2	0	0
3	0	0
4	0	0
5	0	0
6	0	0
7	0	0
8	0	0
9	0	0
10	0	0
11	0	0
12	11	19
13	0	0
14	0	0
15	0	0
16	0	0
17	0	0
18	0	0
19	18	18
20	0	0

As the numbers in column K now run sequentially from 1 up to 19 (or however many times that provider appears) we can now bring in our exclusive list of data where "AAA Ltd" is the provider.

From our Rank column in column K we can write a LOOKUP to pull in the clients serviced by "AAA Ltd". We can put this in column L and give it the heading "AAA Ltd Client List" (I would create a formula for this as AAA Ltd may not always be in first place so in cell L1 I would input **,=J1&" Client List"**, in cell J1 we are looking up the first ranked provider, we then add the words "Client List" at the end so L1 would read "AAA Ltd Client List").

The formula for the LOOKUP in cell L2 would be:

INDEX('Data Sheet'!$B:$B,MATCH(Calcs!$A2,Calcs!K:K,0)) (only use dollar signs where I have used dollar signs as this will help us later).

So bring in the client name from the Data Sheet where you match the number one in column K.

J	K	L
AAA Ltd	Rank	AAA Ltd Client List
0	0	=IFERROR(INDEX('Data Sheet'!$B:$B,MATCH(Calcs!$A2,Calcs!K:K,0)),0)
0	0	
0	0	
0	0	
0	0	
0	0	
0	0	
0	0	
0	0	
0	0	
11	19	
0	0	
0	0	
0	0	
0	0	
0	0	
0	0	
18	18	

Once we are happy the formula is working I would wrap it in an IFERROR:

IFERROR(INDEX('Data Sheet'!$B:$B,MATCH(Calcs!$A2,Calcs!K:K,0))**,0)**

The client it will bring in is:

AAA Ltd	Rank	AAA Ltd Client List
0	0	Henrietta Clemont
0	0	
0	0	
0	0	
0	0	
0	0	
0	0	
0	0	
0	0	
0	0	
11	19	
0	0	
0	0	
0	0	
0	0	
0	0	
0	0	
18	18	
0	0	

Now copy the formula down the column:

AAA Ltd	Rank	AAA Ltd Client List
0	0	Henrietta Clemont
0	0	Jerrilyn Forrestall
0	0	Skye Tittershill
0	0	Art Earry
0	0	Jerrilyn Forrestall
0	0	Hattie Spatig
0	0	Luciana Aucock
0	0	Hattie Spatig
0	0	Marja Blampy
0	0	Van Bourgourd
11	19	Ardelis Walduck
0	0	Sylas McNirlin
0	0	Phaidra Essam
0	0	Marja Blampy
0	0	Tedi Nazaret
0	0	Fallon McDonnell
0	0	Jean Gateley
18	18	Leonidas Sasser
0	0	Kearney Rechert

Now just like with the "Clients" and "Provider" sections of the Calcs sheet, we need to remove the duplicate clients from the list of clients that have completed transactions with AAA Ltd. In cell M1 of the Calcs sheet we would put the header "De Dup", in cell M2 we would put the number one and in cell M3 create the following formula:

IF(COUNTIF(L$2:L3,L3)=1,M2+1,M2) (only use dollar signs where I have used dollar signs as this will help us later).

This formula is looking at the AAA Ltd Client List and saying count how many times the name in the cell L3 appears from L2 to L3. If it only appears once (so the count =1) then add one to the number in the previous cell (so it creates a new number: a unique reference) if it does not equal one, meaning the name has appeared before, use the same number as in the previous cell. So (not a new number, so not unique) as we move down the De Dup column, any time there is a new name the number would increase by one and any time there is a duplicate the number would stay the same. This means that any time there is a new number in the AAA Ltd Client List column of the Calcs sheet there is a corresponding new name in column L of the Calcs sheet.

Once we are happy with the formula wrap it in an IFERROR to return the previous number if an error was found:

IFERROR(IF(COUNTIF(L$2:L3,L3)=1,M2+1,M2),**M2).**

Now copy the formula in cell L3 down to cell L501.

	M
1	De Dup
2	1
3	=IFERROR(IF(COUNTIF(L$2:L3,L3)=1,M2+1,M2),M2)
4	=IFERROR(IF(COUNTIF(L$2:L4,L4)=1,M3+1,M3),M3)
5	=IFERROR(IF(COUNTIF(L$2:L5,L5)=1,M4+1,M4),M4)
6	=IFERROR(IF(COUNTIF(L$2:L6,L6)=1,M5+1,M5),M5)
7	=IFERROR(IF(COUNTIF(L$2:L7,L7)=1,M6+1,M6),M6)
8	=IFERROR(IF(COUNTIF(L$2:L8,L8)=1,M7+1,M7),M7)
9	=IFERROR(IF(COUNTIF(L$2:L9,L9)=1,M8+1,M8),M8)
10	=IFERROR(IF(COUNTIF(L$2:L10,L10)=1,M9+1,M9),M9)
11	=IFERROR(IF(COUNTIF(L$2:L11,L11)=1,M10+1,M10),M10)
12	=IFERROR(IF(COUNTIF(L$2:L12,L12)=1,M11+1,M11),M11)
13	=IFERROR(IF(COUNTIF(L$2:L13,L13)=1,M12+1,M12),M12)
14	=IFERROR(IF(COUNTIF(L$2:L14,L14)=1,M13+1,M13),M13)
15	=IFERROR(IF(COUNTIF(L$2:L15,L15)=1,M14+1,M14),M14)
16	=IFERROR(IF(COUNTIF(L$2:L16,L16)=1,M15+1,M15),M15)
17	=IFERROR(IF(COUNTIF(L$2:L17,L17)=1,M16+1,M16),M16)
18	=IFERROR(IF(COUNTIF(L$2:L18,L18)=1,M17+1,M17),M17)
19	=IFERROR(IF(COUNTIF(L$2:L19,L19)=1,M18+1,M18),M18)
20	=IFERROR(IF(COUNTIF(L$2:L20,L20)=1,M19+1,M19),M19)

As we can see below where Jerrilyn Forrestall and Hattie Spatig appear for the first time, in green, a new number is created that is one greater than the previous number. Where they appear for the second time, in yellow, the number stays the same.

L AAA Ltd Client List	M De Dup
Henrietta Clemont	1
Jerrilyn Forrestall	2
Skye Tittershill	3
Art Earry	4
Jerrilyn Forrestall	4
Hattie Spatig	5
Luciana Aucock	6
Hattie Spatig	6
Marja Blampy	7
Van Bourgourd	8
Ardelis Walduck	9
Sylas McNirlin	10
Phaidra Essam	11

This means that when we run our LOOKUP/INDEX MATCH, we can select unique names only and will have no duplicates in our list. Once you have the formula working I would wrap it in an IFERROR that would return the previous number if an error was found.

In column N of the Calcs sheet we can create a LOOKUP to bring in our unique names as we did in the Dynamic Sheets chapter.

In cell N1, I would type "Clients – Duplicates Removed". The formula for the LOOKUP in cell N2 would be:

INDEX('Data Sheet'!L:L,MATCH(Calcs!$A2,Calcs!M:M,0)) (only use dollar signs where I have used dollar signs as this will help us later). Drag the formula down the sheet.

So bring in the client name from column L of the Calcs sheet where you match the number one in column M of the Calcs sheet.

I would wrap the formula in an IFERROR to return a zero where we could not find any more clients.

IFERROR(INDEX('Data Sheet'!L:L,MATCH(Calcs!$A2,Calcs!M:M,0)),0)

L	M	N	
AAA Ltd Client List	De Dup	Clients - Duplicates Removed	
Henrietta Clemont	1	Henrietta Clemont	
Jerrilyn Forrestall	2	Jerrilyn Forrestall	
Skye Tittershill	3	Skye Tittershill	
Art Earry	4	Art Earry	
Jerrilyn Forrestall	4	Hattie Spatig	
Hattie Spatig	5	Luciana Aucock	
Luciana Aucock	6	Marja Blampy	
Hattie Spatig	6	Van Bourgourd	
Marja Blampy	7	Ardelis Walduck	
Van Bourgourd	8	Sylas McNirlin	
Ardelis Walduck	9	Phaidra Essam	
Sylas McNirlin	10	Tedi Nazaret	
Phaidra Essam	11	Fallon McDonnell	
Marja Blampy	11	Jean Gateley	
Tedi Nazaret	12	Leonidas Sasser	
Fallon McDonnell	13	Kearney Rechert	
Jean Gateley	14		0
Leonidas Sasser	15		0
Kearney Rechert	16		0

We now have our list of clients with the duplicates removed.

As with the providers we can now create a formula to total the revenue for each client and then create a RANK formula to tell us the order from largest to smallest.

In cell O1 we would type "Revenue" and in O2 we need a two-stage formula so we can total the "New Sales" and the "Commission":

SUMIFS('Data Sheet'!$D:$D,'Data Sheet'!$B:$B,Calcs!N2,'Data Sheet'!$G:$G,Calcs!J$1) (only use dollar signs where I have used dollar signs as this will help us later).

Data Sheet $D:$D is the New Sales column.

Data Sheet $B:$B is the name column (Client Name).

Data Sheet $G:$G is the Providers column.

So we want to add up all of the "New Sales" (column D) on the Data Sheet where the client name (column B) on the Data Sheet is equal to the first client in your "Clients – Duplicates" list, cell (N2 of the Calcs sheet), and the "Provider" (column G) on the Data Sheet matches the provider that we are looking at (cell J1: AAA Ltd).

So add the "New Sales" where the client is "Henrietta Clemont" and the provider is "AAA Ltd".

This in turn needs to be added to the total commission using the same criteria, the only thing we change is the column to add up: instead of D in the Data Sheet (the New Sales), we would add column E in the Data Sheet (the Commission), and the formula would look like this:

SUMIFS('Data Sheet'!$E:$E,'Data Sheet'!$B:$B,Calcs!N2,'Data Sheet'!$G:$G,Calcs!J$1)

Data Sheet $E:$E is the Commission column

Data Sheet $B:$B is the name column (Client Name)

Data Sheet $G:$G is the Providers column

In cell O2 we would simply combine the two formulas using the + sign as below

SUMIFS('Data Sheet'!$D:$D,'Data Sheet'!$B:$B,Calcs!N2,'Data Sheet'!$G:$G,Calcs!J$1)+SUMIFS('Data Sheet'!$E:$E,'Data Sheet'!$B:$B,Calcs!N2,'Data Sheet'!$G:$G,Calcs!J$1)

Copy the formula down column O.

In column P we apply a RANK formula to rank the "Total Revenue" numbers we have just calculated in column O.

IF(O2=0,0,RANK(O2,O$2:O$201)) (only use dollar signs where I have used dollar signs as this will help us later).

So if the Total Revenue = 0 we do not want it included in our rank, so put zero, if it does not = 0, rank it among the other numbers in our list.

Copy the formula down the page.

L	M	N		O	P
AAA Ltd Client List	**De Dup**	**Clients - Duplicates Removed**		**Revenue**	**Rank**
Henrietta Clemont	1	Henrietta Clemont		£3,971.00	12
Jerrilyn Forrestall	2	Jerrilyn Forrestall		£15,945.00	1
Skye Tittershill	3	Skye Tittershill		£479.00	16
Art Earry	4	Art Earry		£1,866.00	14
Jerrilyn Forrestall	4	Hattie Spatig		£15,942.00	2
Hattie Spatig	5	Luciana Aucock		£9,558.00	5
Luciana Aucock	6	Marja Blampy		£2,455.00	13
Hattie Spatig	6	Van Bourgourd		£9,115.00	6
Marja Blampy	7	Ardelis Walduck		£8,150.00	8
Van Bourgourd	8	Sylas McNirlin		£7,768.00	9
Ardelis Walduck	9	Phaidra Essam		£8,791.00	7
Sylas McNirlin	10	Tedi Nazaret		£9,846.00	3
Phaidra Essam	11	Fallon McDonnell		£7,674.00	10
Marja Blampy	11	Jean Gateley		£792.00	15
Tedi Nazaret	12	Leonidas Sasser		£4,980.00	11
Fallon McDonnell	13	Kearney Rechert		£9,678.00	4
Jean Gateley	14		0	£0.00	0
Leonidas Sasser	15		0	£0.00	0
Kearney Rechert	16		0	£0.00	0

Now take a deep breath and let's recap!

We now have:

- A **Clients** sheet which lists all our clients in order of revenue and automatically removes the duplicates so each client appears only once. When the data is updated if any new clients appear they will be automatically added and ranked within the list or removed if they no longer appear and as the revenue changes the clients will automatically be re-ranked, and the total will dynamically move up or down with the changes.
- A **Providers** sheet which lists all our providers in order of revenue and automatically removes the duplicates so each provider appears only once. When the data is updated if any new providers appear they will be automatically added and ranked within the list or removed if they no longer appear and as the revenue changes the providers will automatically be re-ranked, and the total will dynamically move up or down with the changes.
- A **Calcs** sheet that has all of the above details for our clients and providers and for our highest ranked provider has all of the clients that make up that providers revenue in rank order as below.

Great work!

This may seem like a lot of work but once complete all you or your client needs to do is update the data, the spreadsheet will do everything else.

If we have put all the dollar signs in the correct places, to create the sections in the Calcs sheet for all the other providers we can simply copy and paste the formulas for our first ranked provider to create all the formulas for our second ranked provider and so on with one small amendment in each.

Copy columns J to P of the Calcs sheet and paste them into columns Q to W:

J	K	L	M	N	O	P
AAA Ltd	Rank	AAA Ltd Client List	De Dup	Clients - Duplicates Removed	Revenue	Rank
0	0	Henrietta Clemont		1 Henrietta Clemont	£3,971.00	12
0	0	Jerrilyn Forrestall		2 Jerrilyn Forrestall	£15,945.00	1
0	0	Skye Tittershill		3 Skye Tittershill	£479.00	16
0	0	Art Earry		4 Art Earry	£1,866.00	14
0	0	Jerrilyn Forrestall		4 Hattie Spatig	£15,942.00	2
0	0	Hattie Spatig		5 Luciana Aucock	£9,558.00	5
0	0	Luciana Aucock		6 Marja Blampy	£2,455.00	13
0	0	Hattie Spatig		6 Van Bourgourd	£9,115.00	6
0	0	Marja Blampy		7 Ardelis Walduck	£8,150.00	8
0	0	Van Bourgourd		8 Sylas McNirlin	£7,768.00	9
11	19	Ardelis Walduck		9 Phaidra Essam	£8,791.00	7
0	0	Sylas McNirlin		10 Tedi Nazaret	£9,846.00	3
0	0	Phaidra Essam		11 Fallon McDonnell	£7,674.00	10
0	0	Marja Blampy		11 Jean Gateley	£792.00	15
0	0	Tedi Nazaret		12 Leonidas Sasser	£4,980.00	11
0	0	Fallon McDonnell		13 Kearney Rechert	£9,678.00	4
0	0	Jean Gateley		14 0	£0.00	0
18	18	Leonidas Sasser		15 0	£0.00	0
0	0	Kearney Rechert		16 0	£0.00	0

Q	R	S	T	U		V	W
AAA Ltd	Rank	AAA Ltd Client List	De Dup	Clients - Duplicates Removed		Revenue	Rank
0	0	Henrietta Clemont	1	Henrietta Clemont		£3,971.00	12
0	0	Jerrilyn Forrestall	2	Jerrilyn Forrestall		£15,945.00	1
0	0	Skye Tittershill	3	Skye Tittershill		£479.00	16
0	0	Art Earry	4	Art Earry		£1,866.00	14
0	0	Jerrilyn Forrestall	4	Hattie Spatig		£15,942.00	2
0	0	Hattie Spatig	5	Luciana Aucock		£9,558.00	5
0	0	Luciana Aucock	6	Marja Blampy		£2,455.00	13
0	0	Hattie Spatig	6	Van Bourgourd		£9,115.00	6
0	0	Marja Blampy	7	Ardelis Walduck		£8,150.00	8
0	0	Van Bourgourd	8	Sylas McNirlin		£7,768.00	9
11	19	Ardelis Walduck	9	Phaidra Essam		£8,791.00	7
0	0	Sylas McNirlin	10	Tedi Nazaret		£9,846.00	3
0	0	Phaidra Essam	11	Fallon McDonnell		£7,674.00	10
0	0	Marja Blampy	11	Jean Gateley		£792.00	15
0	0	Tedi Nazaret	12	Leonidas Sasser		£4,980.00	11
0	0	Fallon McDonnell	13	Kearney Rechert		£9,678.00	4
0	0	Jean Gateley	14		0	£0.00	0
18	18	Leonidas Sasser	15		0	£0.00	0
0	0	Kearney Rechert	16		0	£0.00	0

This will give you the exact same results as for AAA Ltd, your number one ranked provider (if it does not, check your formulas as you must have dollar signs in the wrong place!).

From cell Q1, which is looking for the first ranked provider with the following formula:

=INDEX($G:$G,MATCH($A$2,$I:$I,0))

Bring in the provider in column G where column I matches A2 on the Calcs sheet, A2 was our "Ref" series that ran from one to 200, A2 being one.

As we are now looking for our number *two* ranked provider we simply change A2, which referred to number one to A3, which refers to number *two* as below:

=INDEX($G:$G,MATCH($A$3,$I:$I,0))

The formula now looks for our number two ranked provider, "Service Masters".

Once the change has been made, all the formulas from rows Q to W will update with all the information for our number two ranked provider as below:

Q	R	S	T	U	V	W
Service Masters	Rank	Service Masters Cli	De Dup	Clients - Duplicates Removed	Revenue	Rank
0	0	Libbi Ferronel	1	Libbi Ferronel	£7,082.00	9
0	0	Abagael Nisco	2	Abagael Nisco	£5,407.00	10
3	20	Neddy Lots	3	Neddy Lots	£9,927.00	4
0	0	Edee Kocher	4	Edee Kocher	£5,193.00	11
0	0	Nessa Kettel	5	Nessa Kettel	£12,177.00	2
0	0	Luciana Aucock	6	Luciana Aucock	£8,935.00	7
0	0	Mirabel Clausen	7	Mirabel Clausen	£9,262.00	6
0	0	Jerrilyn Forrestall	8	Jerrilyn Forrestall	£1,135.00	18
0	0	Sawyere McLeoid	9	Sawyere McLeoid	£9,599.00	5
0	0	Alwin Deex	10	Alwin Deex	£13,150.00	1
0	0	Fallon McDonnell	11	Fallon McDonnell	£7,157.00	8
0	0	Mic Kyndred	12	Mic Kyndred	£1,622.00	17
13	19	Demott Sorrell	13	Demott Sorrell	£2,981.00	13
0	0	Kevan Henkens	14	Kevan Henkens	£2,836.00	14
0	0	Dareen Euplate	15	Dareen Euplate	£1,638.00	16
0	0	Leonidas Sasser	16	Leonidas Sasser	£9,969.00	3
0	0	Nessa Kettel	16	Alberto Tibols	£5,012.00	12
0	0	Alberto Tibols	17	Tedi Nazaret	£2,393.00	15
0	0	Alwin Deex	17	0	£0.00	0

Repeat these steps for the other eight providers and increase the $A$2 part of the formula by one for each subsequent provider:

No 1 Ranked Provider Columns **J to P, J1** = INDEX($G:$G,MATCH(**$A$2**,$I:$I,0))

No 2 Ranked Provider Columns **Q to W, Q1** = INDEX($G:$G,MATCH(**$A$3**,$I:$I,0))

No 3 Ranked Provider Columns **X to AD, X1** = INDEX($G:$G,MATCH(**$A$4**,$I:$I,0))

No 4 Ranked Provider Columns **AE to AK, AE1** = INDEX($G:$G,MATCH(**$A$5**,$I:$I,0)

No 5 Ranked Provider Columns **AL to AR, AL1** = INDEX($G:$G,MATCH(**$A$6**,$I:$I,0))

No 6 Ranked Provider Columns **AS to AY, AY1** = INDEX($G:$G,MATCH(**$A$7**,$I:$I,0))

No 7 Ranked Provider Columns **AZ to BF, BF1** = INDEX($G:$G,MATCH(**$A$8**,$I:$I,0))

No 8 Ranked Provider Columns **BG to BM, BG1** = INDEX($G:$G,MATCH(**$A$9**,$I:$I,0))

No 9 Ranked Provider Columns **BN to BT BN1** = INDEX($G:$G,MATCH(**$A$10**,$I:$I,0))

No 10 Ranked Provider Columns **BU to CA BU1** = INDEX($G:$G,MATCH($A$11,$I:$I,0))

I would also put in a few blanks for additional providers on this occasion we will add one so we can see how it works at the end of the exercise.

No 11 Ranked Provider Columns **CB to CH CB1** = INDEX($G:$G,MATCH($A$12,$I:$I,0))

As there is no number eleven ranked provider, this section will show mostly zeros for now.

The last thing to do to complete our Calcs sheet is in column CI (or, if you added more than one blank provider, the next available column) we will type into cell CI1 "Month and Date" and in CI2 insert the following formula:

=MONTH('Data Sheet'!F2)&YEAR('Data Sheet'!F2) (please see the Toolkit for an explanation if required).

This will be needed later for the Provider sheets. From the Date column in the Data Sheet we want the month number from the date in F2 and the year from the date in F2. The date is the 18/01/2020 so the month is January, month one, and the year is 2020 so the formula should return:

12020

Copy the formula down to row 201. We have now completed our Calcs sheet.

Provider Display Pages

To create the display page for the number one ranked provider, AAA Ltd, we need to create a new sheet within the workbook and name it "Provider 1". In cell A1 we want the name of the number one ranked provider, so place an equals sign in cell A1 then go to the Calcs sheet and select cell J1:

=Calcs!J1

In cell A2 we can insert the word "Clients":

In cell A3 we need to bring in the list of clients from the Calcs sheet that is in column N "Clients – Duplicates Removed" for our number one ranked provider.

L	M	N	O	P
AAA Ltd Client List	De Dup	Clients - Duplicates Removed	Revenue	Rank
Henrietta Clemont	1	Henrietta Clemont	£3,971.00	12
Jerrilyn Forrestall	2	Jerrilyn Forrestall	£15,945.00	1
Skye Tittershill	3	Skye Tittershill	£479.00	16
Art Earry	4	Art Earry	£1,866.00	14
Jerrilyn Forrestall	4	Hattie Spatig	£15,942.00	2
Hattie Spatig	5	Luciana Aucock	£9,558.00	5
Luciana Aucock	6	Marja Blampy	£2,455.00	13
Hattie Spatig	6	Van Bourgourd	£9,115.00	6
Marja Blampy	7	Ardelis Walduck	£8,150.00	8
Van Bourgourd	8	Sylas McNirlin	£7,768.00	9
Ardelis Walduck	9	Phaidra Essam	£8,791.00	7
Sylas McNirlin	10	Tedi Nazaret	£9,846.00	3
Phaidra Essam	11	Fallon McDonnell	£7,674.00	10
Marja Blampy	11	Jean Gateley	£792.00	15
Tedi Nazaret	12	Leonidas Sasser	£4,980.00	11
Fallon McDonnell	13	Kearney Rechert	£9,678.00	4
Jean Gateley	14	0	£0.00	0
Leonidas Sasser	15	0	£0.00	0
Kearney Rechert	16	0	£0.00	0
0	17	0	£0.00	0

As we need this in rank order we can use an INDEX MATCH formula as below:

INDEX(Calcs!$N:$N,MATCH(Calcs!$A2,Calcs!$P:$P,0)) (only use dollar signs where I have used dollar signs as this will help us later).

Bring in the client name (for the number one ranked provider) in Calcs column N.

Where we match the number one (Calcs A2) in the rank column in Calcs column P.

This should return Jerrilyn Forrestall as she is the number one ranked client for AAA Ltd by revenue.

We would then wrap this in an IFERROR, returning a zero instead of an error code.

IFERROR(INDEX(Calcs!$N:$N,MATCH(Calcs!$A2,Calcs!$P:$P,0)),0)

Copy the formula down to row 50 (if there are more clients than 50 for any provider, copy the formulas to an appropriate row giving yourself a cushion for any increase in clients going forward).

	A
1	AAA Ltd
2	Clients
3	Jerrilyn Forrestall
4	Hattie Spatig
5	Tedi Nazaret
6	Kearney Rechert
7	Luciana Aucock
8	Van Bourgourd
9	Phaidra Essam
10	Ardelis Walduck
11	Sylas McNirlin
12	Fallon McDonnell
13	Leonidas Sasser
14	Henrietta Clemont
15	Marja Blampy
16	Art Earry
17	Jean Gateley

We now have a dynamic list of clients for our number one ranked provider.

We now need to bring in the revenue per month for each client. In cell B2 insert the date, 01/01/2020 (as my data is from 2020, I have used 2020), then drag this across to column M to give us the 12 months from January to December 2020 (fill the cells with the colour grey). You may need to adjust the formatting to custom "mmm-yy".

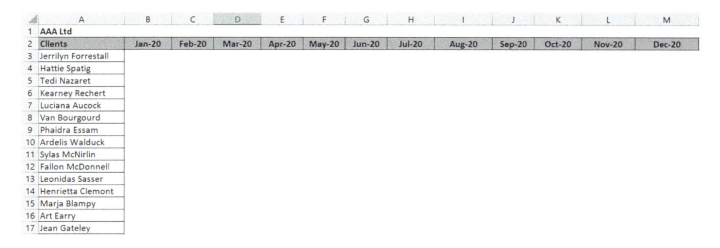

In cell B1 we need a month and year formula so we have the same date format as in column CI of the Calcs sheet:

=MONTH(B2)&YEAR(B2)

Drag the formula across to column M and it should match the results below:

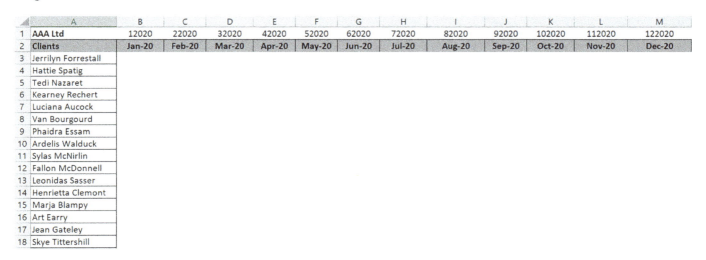

We now need to add up all the revenue each client generated in each month of the year. This is a very similar formula to the revenue formula on the Calcs sheet.

SUMIFS('Data Sheet'!$D:$D,'Data Sheet'!$B:$B,$A3,Calcs!$CI:CI,B1,'Data Sheet'!$G:$G,$A$1)

+SUMIFS('Data Sheet'!$E:$E,'Data Sheet'!$B:$B,$A3,Calcs!$CI:CI,B1,'Data Sheet'!$G:$G,$A$1)

SUMIFS('Data Sheet'!$D:$D,'Data Sheet'!$B:$B,$A3,Calcs!$CI:CI,B1,'Data Sheet'!$G:$G,$A$1) (only use dollar signs where I have used dollar signs as this will help us later).

Data Sheet $D:$D is the New Sales column

Data Sheet $B:$B is the name column (Client Name)

Calcs Sheet $CI:$CI is the Month & Year Column

Data Sheet $G:$G is the Providers Column

So we want to add up all of the New Sales (Column D) on the Data sheet where the Client Name (Column B) on the Data sheet is equal to the first client in your list (Cell A3 Jerrilyn Forrestall), the Month & Year (Column CI of the Calcs sheet) equals the Month & Year of cell B1, and the Provider (Column G) on the Data Sheet matches the Provider that we are looking at (Cell A1 AAA Ltd).

So add the New Sales where the Client is Jerrilyn Forrestall, the Month & DATE is 12020 and the Provider is AAA Ltd.

This in turn needs to be added to the total commission using the same criteria, the only thing we change is the column to add up, instead of column D in the Data sheet (the New Sales) we would add column E in the Data sheet (the Commission) the formula would look like this:

SUMIFS('Data Sheet'!$E:$E,'Data Sheet'!$B:$B,$A3,Calcs!$CI:CI,B1,'Data Sheet'!$G:$G,$A$1) (only use dollar signs where I have used dollar signs as this will help us later)

Data Sheet $E:$E is the Commission Column

Data Sheet $B:$B is the Name Column (Client Name)

Calcs Sheet $CI:$CI is the month and year column

Data Sheet $G:$G is the Providers column

In cell B3 we would simply combine the two formulas using the + sign as below

SUMIFS('Data Sheet'!$D:$D,'Data Sheet'!$B:$B,$A3,Calcs!$CI:CI,B1,'Data Sheet'!$G:$G,$A$1) + SUMIFS('Data Sheet'!$E:$E,'Data Sheet'!$B:$B,$A3,Calcs!$CI:CI,B1,'Data Sheet'!$G:$G,$A$1)

Drag this formula across to cell M. If the dollar signs are in the correct places the only thing that will change as we drag the formula across the page is the date reference B1, so it refers to the different months as it moves across the page:

	A	B	C	D	E	F	G	H	I	J	K	L	M
1	AAA Ltd	12020	22020	32020	42020	52020	62020	72020	82020	92020	102020	112020	122020
2	Clients	Jan-20	Feb-20	Mar-20	Apr-20	May-20	Jun-20	Jul-20	Aug-20	Sep-20	Oct-20	Nov-20	Dec-20
3	Jerrilyn Forrestall	£0.00	£0.00	£0.00	£0.00	£0.00	£0.00	£0.00	£0.00	£0.00	£9,759.00	£6,186.00	£0.00

As above, Jerrilyn Forrestall only had revenue for AAA Ltd in October and November of 2020.

Now copy the formulas in B3 to M3 down to row 50:

	A	B	C	D	E	F	G	H	I	J	K	L	M
1	AAA Ltd	12020	22020	32020	42020	52020	62020	72020	82020	92020	102020	112020	122020
2	Clients	Jan-20	Feb-20	Mar-20	Apr-20	May-20	Jun-20	Jul-20	Aug-20	Sep-20	Oct-20	Nov-20	Dec-20
3	Jerrilyn Forrestall	£0.00	£0.00	£0.00	£0.00	£0.00	£0.00	£0.00	£0.00	£0.00	£9,759.00	£6,186.00	£0.00
4	Hattie Spatig	£0.00	£0.00	£0.00	£0.00	£0.00	£0.00	£0.00	£6,394.00	£0.00	£9,548.00	£0.00	£0.00
5	Tedi Nazaret	£0.00	£0.00	£9,846.00	£0.00	£0.00	£0.00	£0.00	£0.00	£0.00	£0.00	£0.00	£0.00
6	Kearney Rechert	£9,678.00	£0.00	£0.00	£0.00	£0.00	£0.00	£0.00	£0.00	£0.00	£0.00	£0.00	£0.00
7	Luciana Aucock	£0.00	£0.00	£0.00	£0.00	£0.00	£0.00	£0.00	£0.00	£9,558.00	£0.00	£0.00	£0.00
8	Van Bourgourd	£0.00	£0.00	£0.00	£0.00	£0.00	£0.00	£9,115.00	£0.00	£0.00	£0.00	£0.00	£0.00
9	Phaidra Essam	£0.00	£0.00	£0.00	£0.00	£8,791.00	£0.00	£0.00	£0.00	£0.00	£0.00	£0.00	£0.00
10	Ardelis Walduck	£0.00	£0.00	£0.00	£0.00	£0.00	£0.00	£8,150.00	£0.00	£0.00	£0.00	£0.00	£0.00
11	Sylas McNirlin	£0.00	£0.00	£0.00	£0.00	£0.00	£7,768.00	£0.00	£0.00	£0.00	£0.00	£0.00	£0.00
12	Fallon McDonnell	£0.00	£0.00	£7,674.00	£0.00	£0.00	£0.00	£0.00	£0.00	£0.00	£0.00	£0.00	£0.00
13	Leonidas Sasser	£4,980.00	£0.00	£0.00	£0.00	£0.00	£0.00	£0.00	£0.00	£0.00	£0.00	£0.00	£0.00
14	Henrietta Clemont	£0.00	£0.00	£0.00	£0.00	£0.00	£0.00	£0.00	£0.00	£0.00	£0.00	£0.00	£3,971.00
15	Marja Blampy	£0.00	£0.00	£0.00	£1,146.00	£0.00	£0.00	£1,309.00	£0.00	£0.00	£0.00	£0.00	£0.00
16	Art Earry	£0.00	£0.00	£0.00	£0.00	£0.00	£0.00	£0.00	£0.00	£0.00	£0.00	£1,866.00	£0.00
17	Jean Gateley	£0.00	£792.00	£0.00	£0.00	£0.00	£0.00	£0.00	£0.00	£0.00	£0.00	£0.00	£0.00
18	Skye Tittershill	£0.00	£0.00	£0.00	£0.00	£0.00	£0.00	£0.00	£0.00	£0.00	£0.00	£479.00	£0.00
19	0	£0.00	£0.00	£0.00	£0.00	£0.00	£0.00	£0.00	£0.00	£0.00	£0.00	£0.00	£0.00
20	0	£0.00	£0.00	£0.00	£0.00	£0.00	£0.00	£0.00	£0.00	£0.00	£0.00	£0.00	£0.00

We now have a fully dynamic sheet of our number one ranked provider, their clients and their clients' revenue throughout the year that whenever new clients are added, clients are removed, or client revenue is added, it will automatically update and be incorporated into the sheet. But it needs some tidying up.

Firstly, I would like a total for each client in column N (as we did in our Dynamic Sheets chapter with our students). In cell N2, type "Total" and fill it in the colour grey like the rest of the dates.

In cell N3, either select AutoSum or insert the following formula:

SUM(B3:M3)

Copy the formula down to row 50 and fill in grey.

As we did in the Dynamic Sheets chapter, I want to have a total at the bottom of my clients list. We are going to use our "Clients - Duplicates Removed" list in Column N of the Calcs sheet to tell us when we are at the end of our client list. Once we reach the end of our list of names, as the formula is wrapped in an IFERROR it will return a zero when it has no more clients to list. So when we are at the end of our client list, that row will return a zero but the row above it will not so this is where we want our total.

We need to amend the formula in cell A3 from:

INDEX(Calcs!$N:$N,MATCH(Calcs!A2,Calcs!$P:$P,0)),0)

To:

IF(AND(Calcs!N2=0,Calcs!N1<>0),"Total",INDEX(Calcs!N:N,MATCH(Calcs!A2,Calcs!P:P,0))**)**

So if we are at the bottom of our list, insert the word "Total", if not continue with our LOOKUP formula to bring in the client name.

I would now wrap this in an IFERROR copy the formula down to row 50.

IFERROR(IF(AND(Calcs!$N2=0,Calcs!$N1<>0),"Total",INDEX(Calcs!$N:$N,MATCH(Calcs!A2,Calcs!$P:$P,0)))**,0)**

	A	B	C	D	E	F	G	H	I	J	K	L	M	N
1	AAA Ltd	12020	22020	32020	42020	52020	62020	72020	82020	92020	102020	112020	122020	
2	Clients	Jan-20	Feb-20	Mar-20	Apr-20	May-20	Jun-20	Jul-20	Aug-20	Sep-20	Oct-20	Nov-20	Dec-20	Total
3	Jerrilyn Forrestall	£0.00	£0.00	£0.00	£0.00	£0.00	£0.00	£0.00	£0.00	£0.00	£9,759.00	£6,186.00	£0.00	£15,945.00
4	Hattie Spatig	£0.00	£0.00	£0.00	£0.00	£0.00	£0.00	£0.00	£6,394.00	£0.00	£9,548.00	£0.00	£0.00	£15,942.00
5	Tedi Nazaret	£0.00	£0.00	£9,846.00	£0.00	£0.00	£0.00	£0.00	£0.00	£0.00	£0.00	£0.00	£0.00	£9,846.00
6	Kearney Rechert	£9,678.00	£0.00	£0.00	£0.00	£0.00	£0.00	£0.00	£0.00	£0.00	£0.00	£0.00	£0.00	£9,678.00
7	Luciana Aucock	£0.00	£0.00	£0.00	£0.00	£0.00	£0.00	£0.00	£0.00	£9,558.00	£0.00	£0.00	£0.00	£9,558.00
8	Van Bourgourd	£0.00	£0.00	£0.00	£0.00	£0.00	£0.00	£9,115.00	£0.00	£0.00	£0.00	£0.00	£0.00	£9,115.00
9	Phaidra Essam	£0.00	£0.00	£0.00	£0.00	£8,791.00	£0.00	£0.00	£0.00	£0.00	£0.00	£0.00	£0.00	£8,791.00
10	Ardelis Walduck	£0.00	£0.00	£0.00	£0.00	£0.00	£0.00	£8,150.00	£0.00	£0.00	£0.00	£0.00	£0.00	£8,150.00
11	Sylas McNirlin	£0.00	£0.00	£0.00	£0.00	£0.00	£7,768.00	£0.00	£0.00	£0.00	£0.00	£0.00	£0.00	£7,768.00
12	Fallon McDonnell	£0.00	£0.00	£7,674.00	£0.00	£0.00	£0.00	£0.00	£0.00	£0.00	£0.00	£0.00	£0.00	£7,674.00
13	Leonidas Sasser	£4,980.00	£0.00	£0.00	£0.00	£0.00	£0.00	£0.00	£0.00	£0.00	£0.00	£0.00	£0.00	£4,980.00
14	Henrietta Clemont	£0.00	£0.00	£0.00	£0.00	£0.00	£0.00	£0.00	£0.00	£0.00	£0.00	£0.00	£3,971.00	£3,971.00
15	Marja Blampy	£0.00	£0.00	£0.00	£1,146.00	£0.00	£0.00	£1,309.00	£0.00	£0.00	£0.00	£0.00	£0.00	£2,455.00
16	Art Earry	£0.00	£0.00	£0.00	£0.00	£0.00	£0.00	£0.00	£0.00	£0.00	£0.00	£1,866.00	£0.00	£1,866.00
17	Jean Gateley	£0.00	£792.00	£0.00	£0.00	£0.00	£0.00	£0.00	£0.00	£0.00	£0.00	£0.00	£0.00	£792.00
18	Skye Tittershill	£0.00	£0.00	£0.00	£0.00	£0.00	£0.00	£0.00	£0.00	£0.00	£0.00	£479.00	£0.00	£479.00
19	Total	£0.00	£0.00	£0.00	£0.00	£0.00	£0.00	£0.00	£0.00	£0.00	£0.00	£0.00	£0.00	£0.00
20	0	£0.00	£0.00	£0.00	£0.00	£0.00	£0.00	£0.00	£0.00	£0.00	£0.00	£0.00	£0.00	£0.00

We should now have a total under Skye Tittershill, our last client.

We now need each month column to produce a total whenever it finds the word "Total" in column A.

We can do this by amending the formula in cell B4 (not B3) from:

SUMIFS('Data Sheet'!$D:$D,'Data Sheet'!$B:$B,$A4,Calcs!$CI:CI,B1,'Data Sheet'!$G:$G,$A$1)+SUMIFS('Data Sheet'!$E:$E,'Data Sheet'!$B:$B,$A4,Calcs!$CI:CI,B1,'Data Sheet'!$G:$G,$A$1)

To:

IF($A4="Total",SUM(B$3:B3),**SUMIFS('Data Sheet'!$D:$D,'Data Sheet'!$B:$B,$A4,Calcs!CI:CI,B$1,'Data Sheet'!$G:$G,$A$1)+SUMIFS('Data Sheet'!$E:$E,'Data Sheet'!$B:$B,$A4,Calcs!CI:CI,B$1,'Data Sheet'!$G:$G,$A$1))**

We are simply adding an IF formula to say if it finds the word "Total" in the same row in column A, add up everything above it, if not continue with the SUMIF formula it already has. As B$3 in the SUM formula is fixed, it will always add from the first amount (row 3) down wherever "Total" appears in Column A. Ensure that the dollar sign only fixes the number 3 and not the letter B as we need this to move as we drag the formula across the page.

	A	B
1	**AAA Ltd**	12020
2	**Clients**	**Jan-20**
6	Kearney Rechert	£9,678.00
7	Luciana Aucock	£0.00
8	Van Bourgourd	£0.00
9	Phaidra Essam	£0.00
10	Ardelis Walduck	£0.00
11	Sylas McNirlin	£0.00
12	Fallon McDonnell	£0.00
13	Leonidas Sasser	£4,980.00
14	Henrietta Clemont	£0.00
15	Marja Blampy	£0.00
16	Art Earry	£0.00
17	Jean Gateley	£0.00
18	Skye Tittershill	£0.00
19	Total	£14,658.00
20	0	£0.00
21	0	£0.00
22	0	£0.00

Copy the formula from cell B4 to M4 and then copy B4 to M4 down to row 50.

	A	B	C	D	E	F	G	H	I	J	K	L	M	N
1	AAA Ltd	12020	22020	32020	42020	52020	62020	72020	82020	92020	102020	112020	122020	
2	Clients	Jan-20	Feb-20	Mar-20	Apr-20	May-20	Jun-20	Jul-20	Aug-20	Sep-20	Oct-20	Nov-20	Dec-20	Total
9	Phaidra Essam	£0.00	£0.00	£0.00	£0.00	£8,791.00	£0.00	£0.00	£0.00	£0.00	£0.00	£0.00	£0.00	£8,791.00
10	Ardelis Walduck	£0.00	£0.00	£0.00	£0.00	£0.00	£0.00	£8,150.00	£0.00	£0.00	£0.00	£0.00	£0.00	£8,150.00
11	Sylas McNirlin	£0.00	£0.00	£0.00	£0.00	£0.00	£7,768.00	£0.00	£0.00	£0.00	£0.00	£0.00	£0.00	£7,768.00
12	Fallon McDonnell	£0.00	£0.00	£7,674.00	£0.00	£0.00	£0.00	£0.00	£0.00	£0.00	£0.00	£0.00	£0.00	£7,674.00
13	Leonidas Sasser	£4,980.00	£0.00	£0.00	£0.00	£0.00	£0.00	£0.00	£0.00	£0.00	£0.00	£0.00	£0.00	£4,980.00
14	Henrietta Clemont	£0.00	£0.00	£0.00	£0.00	£0.00	£0.00	£0.00	£0.00	£0.00	£0.00	£0.00	£3,971.00	£3,971.00
15	Marja Blampy	£0.00	£0.00	£0.00	£1,146.00	£0.00	£0.00	£1,309.00	£0.00	£0.00	£0.00	£0.00	£0.00	£2,455.00
16	Art Earry	£0.00	£0.00	£0.00	£0.00	£0.00	£0.00	£0.00	£0.00	£0.00	£0.00	£1,866.00	£0.00	£1,866.00
17	Jean Gateley	£0.00	£792.00	£0.00	£0.00	£0.00	£0.00	£0.00	£0.00	£0.00	£0.00	£0.00	£0.00	£792.00
18	Skye Tittershill	£0.00	£0.00	£0.00	£0.00	£0.00	£0.00	£0.00	£0.00	£0.00	£0.00	£479.00	£0.00	£479.00
19	Total	£14,658.00	£792.00	£17,520.00	£1,146.00	£8,791.00	£7,768.00	£18,574.00	£6,394.00	£9,558.00	£19,307.00	£8,531.00	£3,971.00	£117,010.00
20	0	£0.00	£0.00	£0.00	£0.00	£0.00	£0.00	£0.00	£0.00	£0.00	£0.00	£0.00	£0.00	£0.00
21	0	£0.00	£0.00	£0.00	£0.00	£0.00	£0.00	£0.00	£0.00	£0.00	£0.00	£0.00	£0.00	£0.00
22	0	£0.00	£0.00	£0.00	£0.00	£0.00	£0.00	£0.00	£0.00	£0.00	£0.00	£0.00	£0.00	£0.00

We now have a dynamic total line that will move up or down and recalculate the total depending on how many clients are listed in the data.

We are nearly there, now for some conditional formatting.

As in the Dynamic Sheets chapter, we want to hide the zeros that appear under the "Total" line.

Highlight cells A2 to N50 and select conditional formatting from the ribbon, select "New Rule" and then "Use a formula to determine which cells to format".

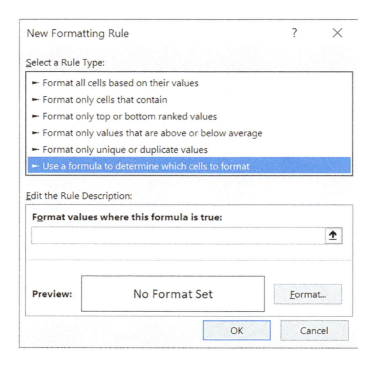

In the formula bar we need to input:

=$A3=0

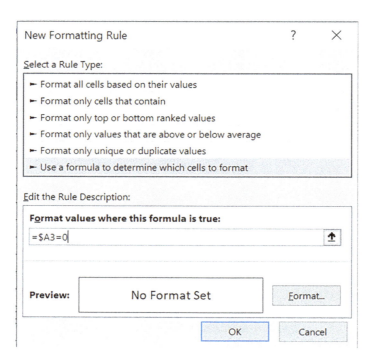

Now select "Format" and change the font from automatic to white.

Select "Border" and change the "Presets" to "None".

Select "Colour" and change to "No Colour".

So anywhere between A3 and A50 equals zero, change the font on that row to white so we can't see it, remove any borders and remove any colour from the cells.

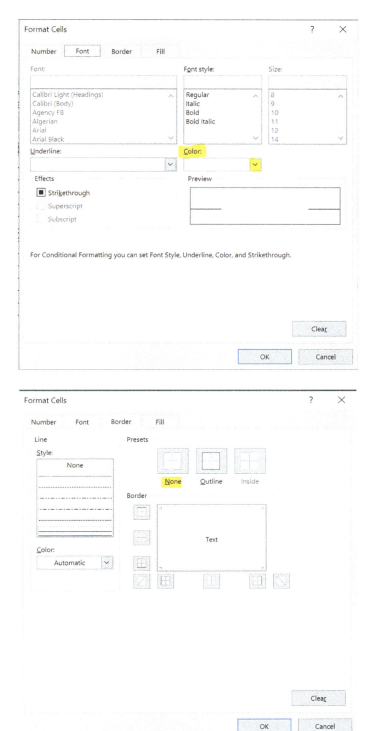

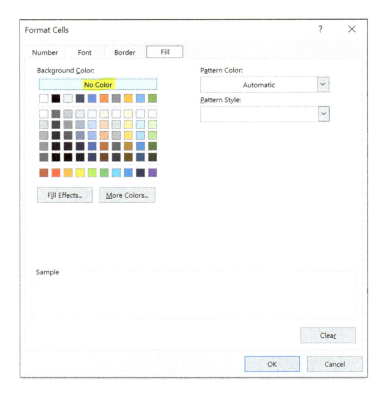

Select "OK" twice to get back to the "New Rule" page.

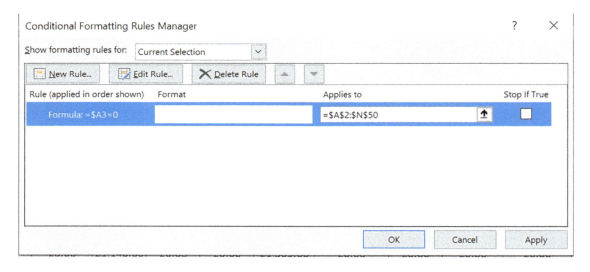

Select "New Rule" and then "Use a formula to determine which cells to format". We should still have cells A3 to A50 highlighted.

In the formula bar input the following formula:

=$A3<>0

Now select "Format" and in "Font" change the font from "Automatic" to "Black".

In "Border" change from "None" to "Outline". Now if there is any row from A3 to A50 that does not have a zero, the font will be black and the cell outlined with a border.

Select "OK" twice and then select apply.

All of the cells below the total line will now have white font, no borders and now not be visible.

The last thing we need to do is highlight our "Total" row in grey.

From the same conditional formatting window select "New Rule" and then "Use a formula to determine which cells to format". We should still have cells A3 to A50 highlighted.

In the formula bar input the following formula:

=$A3="Total"

Now select "Format" and in "Font" change the font from "Automatic" to "Black" and the "Font Style" to "Bold".

Now select "Fill" and select a medium grey from the colour chart.

Press "OK" twice and then select "Apply".

To finish up I would highlight cells B1 to M1 and change the font to white.

	A	B	C	D	E	F	G	H	I	J	K	L	M	N
1	AAA Ltd													
2	Clients	Jan-20	Feb-20	Mar-20	Apr-20	May-20	Jun-20	Jul-20	Aug-20	Sep-20	Oct-20	Nov-20	Dec-20	Total
3	Jerrilyn Forrestall	£0.00	£0.00	£0.00	£0.00	£0.00	£0.00	£0.00	£0.00	£0.00	£9,759.00	£6,186.00	£0.00	£15,945.00
4	Hattie Spatig	£0.00	£0.00	£0.00	£0.00	£0.00	£0.00	£0.00	£6,394.00	£0.00	£9,548.00	£0.00	£0.00	£15,942.00
5	Tedi Nazaret	£0.00	£0.00	£9,846.00	£0.00	£0.00	£0.00	£0.00	£0.00	£0.00	£0.00	£0.00	£0.00	£9,846.00
6	Kearney Rechert	£9,678.00	£0.00	£0.00	£0.00	£0.00	£0.00	£0.00	£0.00	£0.00	£0.00	£0.00	£0.00	£9,678.00
7	Luciana Aucock	£0.00	£0.00	£0.00	£0.00	£0.00	£0.00	£0.00	£0.00	£9,558.00	£0.00	£0.00	£0.00	£9,558.00
8	Van Bourgourd	£0.00	£0.00	£0.00	£0.00	£0.00	£0.00	£9,115.00	£0.00	£0.00	£0.00	£0.00	£0.00	£9,115.00
9	Phaidra Essam	£0.00	£0.00	£0.00	£0.00	£8,791.00	£0.00	£0.00	£0.00	£0.00	£0.00	£0.00	£0.00	£8,791.00
10	Ardelis Walduck	£0.00	£0.00	£0.00	£0.00	£0.00	£0.00	£8,150.00	£0.00	£0.00	£0.00	£0.00	£0.00	£8,150.00
11	Sylas McNirlin	£0.00	£0.00	£0.00	£0.00	£0.00	£7,768.00	£0.00	£0.00	£0.00	£0.00	£0.00	£0.00	£7,768.00
12	Fallon McDonnell	£0.00	£0.00	£7,674.00	£0.00	£0.00	£0.00	£0.00	£0.00	£0.00	£0.00	£0.00	£0.00	£7,674.00
13	Leonidas Sasser	£4,980.00	£0.00	£0.00	£0.00	£0.00	£0.00	£0.00	£0.00	£0.00	£0.00	£0.00	£0.00	£4,980.00
14	Henrietta Clemont	£0.00	£0.00	£0.00	£0.00	£0.00	£0.00	£0.00	£0.00	£0.00	£0.00	£0.00	£3,971.00	£3,971.00
15	Marja Blampy	£0.00	£0.00	£0.00	£1,146.00	£0.00	£0.00	£1,309.00	£0.00	£0.00	£0.00	£0.00	£0.00	£2,455.00
16	Art Earry	£0.00	£0.00	£0.00	£0.00	£0.00	£0.00	£0.00	£0.00	£0.00	£0.00	£1,866.00	£0.00	£1,866.00
17	Jean Gateley	£0.00	£792.00	£0.00	£0.00	£0.00	£0.00	£0.00	£0.00	£0.00	£0.00	£0.00	£0.00	£792.00
18	Skye Tittershill	£0.00	£0.00	£0.00	£0.00	£0.00	£0.00	£0.00	£0.00	£0.00	£0.00	£479.00	£0.00	£479.00
19	Total	£14,658.00	£792.00	£17,520.00	£1,146.00	£8,791.00	£7,768.00	£18,574.00	£6,394.00	£9,558.00	£19,307.00	£8,531.00	£3,971.00	£117,010.00
20														

We should now have a tidy worksheet.

We now need to make ten copies of our "Provider 1" sheet and label them Provider 2 to Provider 11. We then need to make some minor modifications to column A on each sheet.

On sheet "Provider 2" we need to amend the formula in cell A1 to look for the number two ranked provider instead of the number one ranked provider.

From: =INDEX(Calcs!G:G,MATCH(1,Calcs!I:I,0))

To: =INDEX(Calcs!G:G,MATCH(2,Calcs!I:I,0))

For each subsequent provider, we increase the number we are matching by one; this will bring in the number two ranked provider "Service Masters".

Now in cell A3 of the "Provider 2" sheet we need to change this formula from:

=IFERROR(IF(AND(Calcs!$N2=0,Calcs!$N1<>0),"Total",INDEX(Calcs!$N:$N,MATCH(Calcs!A2,Calcs!$P:$P,0))),0)

Calcs!$N:$N is the "Clients - Duplicates Removed" column for the number one ranked provider.

Calcs!$P:$P is the "Rank" column for the number one ranked provider.

To:

=IFERROR(IF(AND(Calcs!$U2=0,Calcs!$U1<>0),"Total",INDEX(Calcs!$U:$U,MATCH(Calcs!A2,Calcs!$W:$W,0))),0)

The easiest way to do this would be to use the find and replace tool, ensuring that you include the dollar signs in what you are replacing, e.g. replace "$N" with "$U" to ensure that only an N with a dollar sign in front of it gets changed. This will ensure that only the formulas are changed not the text and replace "$P" with "$W" ensuring only a P with a dollar sign in front of it will be changed.

This will now use the "Clients - Duplicate Removed" and "Rank" columns of the number two ranked provider.

Repeat these steps for the other provider columns as below:

Provider 1 - IFERROR(IF(AND(Calcs!$N2=0,Calcs!$N1<>0),"Total",INDEX(Calcs!$N:$N,MATCH(Calcs!A2,Calcs!$P:$P,0))),0)

Provider 2 - IFERROR(IF(AND(Calcs!$U2=0,Calcs!$U1<>0),"Total",INDEX(Calcs!$U:$U,MATCH(Calcs!A2,Calcs!$W:$W,0))),0)

Provider 3 - IFERROR(IF(AND(Calcs!$AB2=0,Calcs!$AB1<>0),"Total",INDEX(Calcs!$AB:$AB,MATCH(Calcs!A2,Calcs!$AD:$AD,0))),0)

Provider 4 - IFERROR(IF(AND(Calcs!$AI2=0,Calcs!$AI1<>0),"Total",INDEX(Calcs!$AI:$AI,MATCH(Calcs!A2,Calcs!$AK:$AK,0))),0)

Provider 5 - IFERROR(IF(AND(Calcs!$AP2=0,Calcs!$AP1<>0),"Total",INDEX(Calcs!$AP:$AP,MATCH(Calcs!A2,Calcs!$AR:$AR,0))),0)

Provider 6 - IFERROR(IF(AND(Calcs!$AW2=0,Calcs!$AW1<>0),"Total",INDEX(Calcs!$AW:$AW,MATCH(Calcs!A2, Calcs!$AY:$AY,0))),0)

Provider 7 - IFERROR(IF(AND(Calcs!$BD2=0,Calcs!$BD1<>0),"Total",INDEX(Calcs!$BD:$BD,MATCH(Calcs!A2,Calcs! $BF:$BF,0))),0)

Provider 8 - IFERROR(IF(AND(Calcs!$BK2=0,Calcs!$BK1<>0),"Total",INDEX(Calcs!$BK:$BK,MATCH(Calcs!A2,Calcs! $BM:$BM,0))),0)

Provider 9 - IFERROR(IF(AND(Calcs!$BR2=0,Calcs!$BR1<>0),"Total",INDEX(Calcs!$BR:$BR,MATCH(Calcs!A2,Calcs! $BT:$BT,0))),0)

Provider 10 - IFERROR(IF(AND(Calcs!$BY2=0,Calcs!$BY1<>0),"Total",INDEX(Calcs!$BY:$BY,MATCH(Calcs!A2,Calcs! $CA:$CA,0))),0)

Provider 11 - IFERROR(IF(AND(Calcs!$CF2=0,Calcs!$CF1<>0),"Total",INDEX(Calcs!$CF:$CF,MATCH(Calcs!A2,Calcs! $CH:$CH,0))),0)

The project is now complete. We should have a "Provider 11" sheet that shows blank. Now go to the Data Sheet and change the provider name in row 4 from "Service Masters" to "Spare Provider" as below:

	A	B	C	D	E	F	G
1	Costomer ID	Name	email	New Sa	Commission	Date	Providers
2		1038 Bertrand McIllrick	bmcillrick11@sun.com	£749.00	£128.00	02/01/2020	Self Service Providers
3		1034 Hyacinthie Gullam	hgullamx@wordpress.com	£6,317.00	£115.00	04/01/2020	Ace Sales
4		1024 Tedi Nazaret	tnazaretn@123-reg.co.uk	£2,391.00	£2.00	05/01/2020	Spare Provider
5		1002 Filide Makeswell	fmakeswell1@tamu.edu	£998.00	£198.00	07/01/2020	Exclusive Products
6		1011 Brnaba Benoy	bbenoya@tuttocitta.it	£8,204.00	£56.00	07/01/2020	Premier Service
7		1021 Henrietta Clemont	hclemontk@npr.org	£5,275.00	£189.00	08/01/2020	Design Kings
8		1002 Filide Makeswell	fmakeswell1@tamu.edu	£8,003.00	£146.00	09/01/2020	A1 Sales

Now if we check the Provider sheet we will see that "Spare Provider" has been added to the bottom of the list of providers:

	A	B	C	D	E
1		New Sales	Commission	Total	%
2	AAA Ltd	£114,854.00	£2,156.00	£117,010.00	12.07%
3	Service Masters	£111,127.00	£1,955.00	£113,082.00	11.66%
4	Premier Service	£103,378.00	£1,659.00	£105,037.00	10.83%
5	JJ's Products	£100,263.00	£2,017.00	£102,280.00	10.55%
6	Exclusive Products	£96,017.00	£1,893.00	£97,910.00	10.10%
7	The Professionals	£92,557.00	£2,301.00	£94,858.00	9.78%
8	Self Service Providers	£88,366.00	£2,324.00	£90,690.00	9.35%
9	Ace Sales	£88,961.00	£1,729.00	£90,690.00	9.35%
10	A1 Sales	£80,960.00	£2,366.00	£83,326.00	8.60%
11	Design Kings	£69,844.00	£2,342.00	£72,186.00	7.45%
12	Spare Provider	£2,391.00	£2.00	£2,393.00	0.25%
13	Total	£948,718.00	£20,744.00	£969,462.00	100.00%

If we now check the Provider 11 sheet we will now see that it has been populated with Spare Provider's only client, Tedi Nazaret.

	A	B	C	D	E	F	G	H	I	J	K	L	M	N
1	Spare Provider													
2	Clients	Jan-20	Feb-20	Mar-20	Apr-20	May-20	Jun-20	Jul-20	Aug-20	Sep-20	Oct-20	Nov-20	Dec-20	Total
3	Tedi Nazaret	£2,393.00	£0.00	£0.00	£0.00	£0.00	£0.00	£0.00	£0.00	£0.00	£0.00	£0.00	£0.00	£2,393.00
4	Total	£2,393.00	£0.00	£0.00	£0.00	£0.00	£0.00	£0.00	£0.00	£0.00	£0.00	£0.00	£0.00	£2,393.00

If we go back to the Data Sheet and change the amount in the New Sales column in row 4 from £2,391.00 to £1,000,000.00:

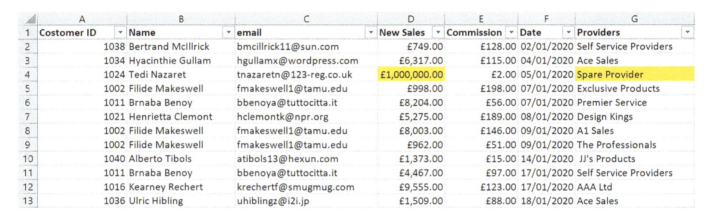

	A	B	C	D	E	F	G
1	Costomer ID	Name	email	New Sales	Commission	Date	Providers
2	1038	Bertrand McIllrick	bmcillrick11@sun.com	£749.00	£128.00	02/01/2020	Self Service Providers
3	1034	Hyacinthie Gullam	hgullamx@wordpress.com	£6,317.00	£115.00	04/01/2020	Ace Sales
4	1024	Tedi Nazaret	tnazaretn@123-reg.co.uk	£1,000,000.00	£2.00	05/01/2020	Spare Provider
5	1002	Filide Makeswell	fmakeswell1@tamu.edu	£998.00	£198.00	07/01/2020	Exclusive Products
6	1011	Brnaba Benoy	bbenoya@tuttocitta.it	£8,204.00	£56.00	07/01/2020	Premier Service
7	1021	Henrietta Clemont	hclemontk@npr.org	£5,275.00	£189.00	08/01/2020	Design Kings
8	1002	Filide Makeswell	fmakeswell1@tamu.edu	£8,003.00	£146.00	09/01/2020	A1 Sales
9	1002	Filide Makeswell	fmakeswell1@tamu.edu	£962.00	£51.00	09/01/2020	The Professionals
10	1040	Alberto Tibols	atibols13@hexun.com	£1,373.00	£15.00	14/01/2020	JJ's Products
11	1011	Brnaba Benoy	bbenoya@tuttocitta.it	£4,467.00	£97.00	17/01/2020	Self Service Providers
12	1016	Kearney Rechert	krechertf@smugmug.com	£9,555.00	£123.00	17/01/2020	AAA Ltd
13	1036	Ulric Hibling	uhiblingz@i2i.jp	£1,509.00	£88.00	18/01/2020	Ace Sales

Spare Provider now automatically moves to the top of the list of providers:

	A	B	C	D	E
1		New Sales	Commission	Total	%
2	Spare Provider	£1,000,000.00	£2.00	£1,000,002.00	50.84%
3	AAA Ltd	£114,854.00	£2,156.00	£117,010.00	5.95%
4	Service Masters	£111,127.00	£1,955.00	£113,082.00	5.75%
5	Premier Service	£103,378.00	£1,659.00	£105,037.00	5.34%
6	JJ's Products	£100,263.00	£2,017.00	£102,280.00	5.20%
7	Exclusive Products	£96,017.00	£1,893.00	£97,910.00	4.98%
8	The Professionals	£92,557.00	£2,301.00	£94,858.00	4.82%
9	Self Service Providers	£88,366.00	£2,324.00	£90,690.00	4.61%
10	Ace Sales	£88,961.00	£1,729.00	£90,690.00	4.61%
11	A1 Sales	£80,960.00	£2,366.00	£83,326.00	4.24%
12	Design Kings	£69,844.00	£2,342.00	£72,186.00	3.67%
13	Total	£1,946,327.00	£20,744.00	£1,967,071.00	100.00%

And it now appears (as it is the number one ranked provider) in the Provider 1 sheet:

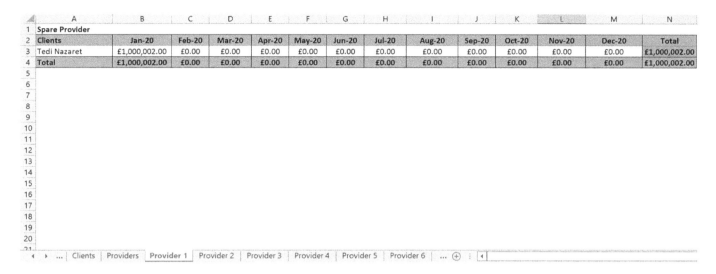

	A	B	C	D	E	F	G	H	I	J	K	L	M	N
1	Spare Provider													
2	Clients	Jan-20	Feb-20	Mar-20	Apr-20	May-20	Jun-20	Jul-20	Aug-20	Sep-20	Oct-20	Nov-20	Dec-20	Total
3	Tedi Nazaret	£1,000,002.00	£0.00	£0.00	£0.00	£0.00	£0.00	£0.00	£0.00	£0.00	£0.00	£0.00	£0.00	£1,000,002.00
4	Total	£1,000,002.00	£0.00	£0.00	£0.00	£0.00	£0.00	£0.00	£0.00	£0.00	£0.00	£0.00	£0.00	£1,000,002.00

Clients | Providers | Provider 1 | Provider 2 | Provider 3 | Provider 4 | Provider 5 | Provider 6

Our spreadsheet is now fully dynamic and will incorporate or remove new or removed clients and providers, change the order they are displayed in sheet by sheet and re-rank them in the Client and Provider lists based on their changing revenue. No buttons, refreshing or pivot tables are required.

The system we have just used can be applied to any data set and after a little practice you will get quicker and quicker at it. As with anything, when using Excel the speed of the tool will depend on the size of your data set and the power of your machine.

It is now time to pass on the baton to see how much further you can take it, over the years I have found numerous applications for my Double Rank method and I am still finding new ways to use it today. Now it is over to you!

Tool Kit Examples

In order to fully utilise the techniques in the following chapters we will need certain tools:

Basic Tools:

IF Formulas

SUMIFS

Fixed references or $ signs

Month

Year

Rank Formulas

Data Validation\Drop down lists

Advanced Tools:

Multiple or Nested IF Formulas

IF/AND formulas

Rank Tie Breaker formulas

IFERROR formulas

INDEX MATCH formulas

For any formula we must start with an "=" to tell Excel we are asking it to calculate something for us.

When we refer to any text in a formula, as opposed to numbers, we need to put it in double speech marks "Insert Text".

IF Formulas

I believe IF formulas are the most powerful formulas in Excel, simply because you can add it to any other formula to apply a condition, or multiple conditions, to it.

The table below show the conditions that can be applied to an IF formula.

Conditions		
>	Greater Than	20 > 10
<	Less Than	10 < 20
=	Equal To	20 = 20
<>	Not Equal To	20 <> 10

I always find it easier to create an IF formula if I say it first as an IF statement in Excel is pretty much the same as a conditional statement that you would say.

A single IF statement is made up of three stages only:

1. The Condition
2. What happens if the condition is met or True
3. What happens if the condition is NOT met or False

After we have finished each stage of the formula, we must insert a comma to tell Excel we are ready to move on to the next stage until we get to the end of the formula for which we use a close bracket (parenthesis).

Below is a statement as we would say it, but it translates easily into a formula:

IF You Keep Skipping School, You are Going to Get Expelled, if You Don't Skip You Can Stay In School

IF = A Conditional Instruction

Blue = The Condition

Red = The Result if the Condition is Met or True

Green = The Result if the condition is NOT met or False

If we were to say the above statement out loud, we would naturally pause after each section, this would help to tell us where the commas should go in our formula.

Although the above statement could never be used in Excel, it is useful to see what it would look like.

So we start with the equals sign, then we type IF and an open bracket as below:

=IF(You Keep Skipping School,You are Going to Get Expelled,if You Stop You Can Stay In School)

In the below table we need to establish which classrooms the various students will be taking their classes in. We know that Teacher 1 will be in Classroom A and everyone else will be in Classroom B.

Teachers	Students
Teacher 1	Adam
Teacher 1	Bella
Teacher 3	Charles
Teacher 1	Donna
Teacher 3	Etnan
Teacher 2	Fiona
Teacher 3	Michael
Teacher 3	Craig
Teacher 1	Terry
Teacher 3	Katrina
Teacher 2	Mary

Our formula would sound like this:

=if(The Teacher ="Teacher 1", Enter "Classroom A", If it is Not "Teacher 1" Enter "The Hall")

And the formula would look like this:

=if(A2="Teacher 1","Classroom A","The Hall")

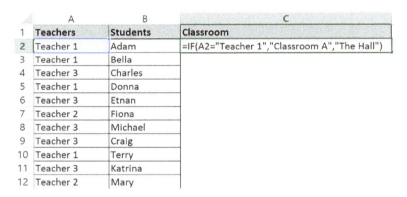

We would then drag or copy the formula down to work out where the rest of the students will be studying. The result should look like this:

	A	B	C
1	**Teachers**	**Students**	**Classroom**
2	Teacher 1	Adam	Classroom A
3	Teacher 1	Bella	Classroom A
4	Teacher 3	Charles	The Hall
5	Teacher 1	Donna	Classroom A
6	Teacher 3	Etnan	The Hall
7	Teacher 2	Fiona	The Hall
8	Teacher 3	Michael	The Hall
9	Teacher 3	Craig	The Hall
10	Teacher 1	Terry	Classroom A
11	Teacher 3	Katrina	The Hall
12	Teacher 2	Mary	The Hall

SUMIFs

To SUM (add) a range of numbers based on a condition or multiple conditions being met.

Unlike a standard IF formula this will look at a range of data rather than just one cell:

	A	B
1	Students	Fees
2	Adam	£100
3	Bella	£100
4	Charles	£100
5	Donna	£100
6	Etnan	£100
7	Fiona	£100
8	Michael	£100
9	Adam	£100
10	Adam	£100
11	Katrina	£100
12	Mary	£100
13	Adam	£100
14	Bella	£100
15	Charles	£100

How would we calculate the amount of fees that Adam owes?

To find Adam's total, we need to set a condition and say what happens if the condition is met.

Our formula would sound like this:

=**SUMIFS**(The Column range containing the numbers we want to add, The column range with the criteria we need to match, the name or item we are looking to match)

And the formula would look like this:

=**SUMIF**(B2:B15,A2:A15,"Adam")

SUMIF, The Range of Data we want to Add up (B2:B15), The Range of Data that contains our condition(A2:15),The condition("Adam")

As this is a SUM formula we do not have to tell it what to do if the condition is *not* met as it will just not include that number or those numbers into the sum.

SUMIFS(Sum Range,Condition Range,Condition)

SUMIFS(B2:B15,A2:A15,"Adam")

Fixed References or $ Signs

With any formula we will be looking at or referring to a specific cell or cells. In the previous IF example the first formula we created was looking at cell A2.

	A	B	C
1	**Teachers**	**Students**	**Classroom**
2	Teacher 1	Adam	=IF(A2="Teacher 1","Classroom A","The Hall")
3	Teacher 1	Bella	
4	Teacher 3	Charles	
5	Teacher 1	Donna	
6	Teacher 3	Etnan	
7	Teacher 2	Fiona	
8	Teacher 3	Michael	
9	Teacher 3	Craig	
10	Teacher 1	Terry	
11	Teacher 3	Katrina	
12	Teacher 2	Mary	

However, once we drag the formula down or move the formula, Excel will make the assumption that we want to change the cell that we are looking at. So when the formula moves down one row to row 3, Excel automatically changes the formula to look at cell A3 instead of A2 and when the formula moves to A4 it automatically changes what the formula is looking at to A4 and so on.

This also works when moving a formula left or right, Excel will automatically change the letter as well to B or C, or wherever you have moved the formula to.

	A	B	C
1	**Teachers**	**Students**	**Classroom**
2	Teacher 1	Adam	=IF(A2="Teacher 1","Classroom A","The Hall")
3	Teacher 1	Bella	=IF(A3="Teacher 1","Classroom A","The Hall")
4	Teacher 3	Charles	=IF(A4="Teacher 1","Classroom A","The Hall")
5	Teacher 1	Donna	=IF(A5="Teacher 1","Classroom A","The Hall")
6	Teacher 3	Etnan	=IF(A6="Teacher 1","Classroom A","The Hall")
7	Teacher 2	Fiona	=IF(A7="Teacher 1","Classroom A","The Hall")
8	Teacher 3	Michael	=IF(A8="Teacher 1","Classroom A","The Hall")
9	Teacher 3	Craig	=IF(A9="Teacher 1","Classroom A","The Hall")
10	Teacher 1	Terry	=IF(A10="Teacher 1","Classroom A","The Hall")
11	Teacher 3	Katrina	=IF(A11="Teacher 1","Classroom A","The Hall")
12	Teacher 2	Mary	=IF(A12="Teacher 1","Classroom A","The Hall")

In this example it is exactly what we want Excel to do, but what if we don't want our cell references to change?

In the example below we have added an input box in column C1 as our teachers each get to use Classroom A on rotation so when it is the turn of Teacher 2 to have Classroom A they can change the name in the input box which will directly affect the formula as below. The formula now reads:

=IF(A4=**C1**,"Classsroom A","The Hall")

	A	B	C
1			Teacher 1
2			
3	Teachers	Students	Classroom
4	Teacher 1	Adam	=IF(A4=C1,"Classroom A","The Hall")
5	Teacher 1	Bella	
6	Teacher 3	Charles	
7	Teacher 1	Donna	
8	Teacher 3	Etnan	
9	Teacher 2	Fiona	
10	Teacher 3	Michael	
11	Teacher 3	Craig	
12	Teacher 1	Terry	
13	Teacher 3	Katrina	
14	Teacher 2	Mary	

If we were to now drag our formulas down we would have a problem as Excel will change our formula from C1, our input box, to C2, which is blank and continue moving down to cells that we do not want as they do not have the information we are looking for.

	A	B	C
1			Teacher 1
2			
3	Teachers	Students	Classroom
4	Teacher 1	Adam	=IF(A4=C1,"Classroom A","The Hall")
5	Teacher 1	Bella	=IF(A5=C2,"Classroom A","The Hall")
6	Teacher 3	Charles	=IF(A6=C3,"Classroom A","The Hall")
7	Teacher 1	Donna	=IF(A7=C4,"Classroom A","The Hall")
8	Teacher 3	Etnan	=IF(A8=C5,"Classroom A","The Hall")
9	Teacher 2	Fiona	=IF(A9=C6,"Classroom A","The Hall")
10	Teacher 3	Michael	=IF(A10=C7,"Classroom A","The Hall")
11	Teacher 3	Craig	=IF(A11=C8,"Classroom A","The Hall")
12	Teacher 1	Terry	=IF(A12=C9,"Classroom A","The Hall")
13	Teacher 3	Katrina	=IF(A13=C10,"Classroom A","The Hall")
14	Teacher 2	Mary	=IF(A14=C11,"Classroom A","The Hall")

The way to overcome this is by placing a dollar sign in front of either the number or letter that you want to fix in place, in this case the 1 in C1 as below:

C$1

=IF(A4=C$1,"Classroom A","The Hall")

	A	B	C
1			Teacher 1
2			
3	Teachers	Students	Classroom
4	Teacher 1	Adam	=IF(A4=C$1,"Classroom A","The Hall")
5	Teacher 1	Bella	=IF(A5=C$1,"Classroom A","The Hall")
6	Teacher 3	Charles	=IF(A6=C$1,"Classroom A","The Hall")
7	Teacher 1	Donna	=IF(A7=C$1,"Classroom A","The Hall")
8	Teacher 3	Etnan	=IF(A8=C$1,"Classroom A","The Hall")
9	Teacher 2	Fiona	=IF(A9=C$1,"Classroom A","The Hall")
10	Teacher 3	Michael	=IF(A10=C$1,"Classroom A","The Hall")
11	Teacher 3	Craig	=IF(A11=C$1,"Classroom A","The Hall")
12	Teacher 1	Terry	=IF(A12=C$1,"Classroom A","The Hall")
13	Teacher 3	Katrina	=IF(A13=C$1,"Classroom A","The Hall")
14	Teacher 2	Mary	=IF(A14=C$1,"Classroom A","The Hall")

Now our formula continues to look at C1 and can now work how we want it to:

	A	B	C
1			Teacher 1
2			
3	Teachers	Students	Classroom
4	Teacher 1	Adam	Classroom A
5	Teacher 1	Bella	Classroom A
6	Teacher 3	Charles	The Hall
7	Teacher 1	Donna	Classroom A
8	Teacher 3	Etnan	The Hall
9	Teacher 2	Fiona	The Hall
10	Teacher 3	Michael	The Hall
11	Teacher 3	Craig	The Hall
12	Teacher 1	Terry	Classroom A
13	Teacher 3	Katrina	The Hall
14	Teacher 2	Mary	The Hall

If we wanted to make sure that our formula looked at C1 wherever we moved our formula, including left and right, we would create an "absolute reference" by placing a dollar sign in front of both the number and the letter.

$C$1

Month

When we need to compress a series of individual dates into months, we can use a Month formula. We simply refer to the cell with the date in and use the following formula.

=Month(A1)

From the diagram below we can see that if we place this formula in cell B1 this will return the number of the month one for January up to 12 for December, in this case two for February:

A	B
01/02/2022	2

Year

When we need to compress a series of individual dates into years we can use a Year formula. We simply refer to the cell with the date in and use the following formula.

=Year(A1)

From the diagram below we can see that if we place this formula in cell B1 this will return the full year of the date, in this case 2022:

A	B
01/02/2022	2022

I would typically add the two formulas together using an ampersand (or "and" sign) "&":

=Month(A1)&Year(A1)

This would join the two results from the two formulas as below:

A	B
01/02/2022	22022

This means we can identify all of the dates in any month or year.

Rank Formulas

A Rank formula will give the numerical position (1st, 2nd, 3rd etc.) to a number in a series of other numbers as below:

Rank Ascending

10	Rank order	3
20	Rank order	2
30	Rank order	1

Rank Descending would be the opposite in that it would give the lowest number as first and the highest number as last.

In the table below we have a number of exam results where we want to rank the results to tell us who got the top score and who got the worst:

	A	B
1	**Student**	**Score**
2	Adam	75.00%
3	Bella	40.00%
4	Charles	60.00%
5	Donna	45.00%
6	Etnan	25.00%
7	Fiona	51.00%
8	Michael	33.00%
9	Craig	28.00%
10	Terry	92.00%
11	Katrina	78.00%
12	Mary	54.00%

Our rank formula would look like this:

Rank(The number you wish to rank,The range you wish to rank it in,The Rank Order)

=Rank(B2,$B2:B12)

If we leave out the order Excel will automatically rank in descending order, if we wanted ascending order we would add a coma and 1: =Rank(B2,B2:B12,1)

As we are going to move this formula down, but we always want the range B2:B12 to remain the same, we would add dollar signs to fix our reference.

=Rank(B2,B$2:B$12)

	A	B	C
1	Student	Score	
2	Adam	75%	RANK(B2,B$2:B$12)
3	Bella	40%	RANK(B3,B$2:B$12)
4	Charles	60%	RANK(B4,B$2:B$12)
5	Donna	45%	RANK(B5,B$2:B$12)
6	Etnan	25%	RANK(B6,B$2:B$12)
7	Fiona	51%	RANK(B7,B$2:B$12)
8	Michael	33%	RANK(B8,B$2:B$12)
9	Craig	28%	RANK(B9,B$2:B$12)
10	Terry	92%	RANK(B10,B$2:B$12)
11	Katrina	78%	RANK(B11,B$2:B$12)
12	Mary	54%	RANK(B12,B$2:B$12)

	A	B	C
1	Student	Score	Rank
2	Adam	75%	3
3	Bella	40%	8
4	Charles	60%	4
5	Donna	45%	7
6	Etnan	25%	11
7	Fiona	51%	6
8	Michael	33%	9
9	Craig	28%	10
10	Terry	92%	1
11	Katrina	78%	2
12	Mary	54%	5

So you can see the number one rank is given to Terry with 92%, and the lowest to Etnan at 25%.

Data Validation/Drop Down Lists

Data validation lists allow you to control or validate what can be input by the user of your spreadsheet. In most cases when you are using formulas you will be looking for or relying on specific information, for example if you had a student called "Thomas" and you created a formula to look for "Thomas", if the user had used "Tom" or "Tommy" your formula would not pick it up as the names differ.

If we wanted to create a validation list of my students below:

We would either select the cell or cell range that we want to control with data validation and then from the ribbon at the top of the page select Data and from the Data Tools section select Data Validation.

From the drop-down menu select Data Validation and it should look like this:

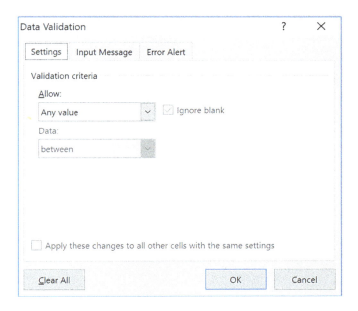

In the "Allow" box which will default to "Any Value" select List, and in the Source box that appears select your list of students A1 to A12. You will notice that Excel creates an absolute reference by adding a dollar sign before each letter and each number so wherever we put the validation list the source will remain the same.

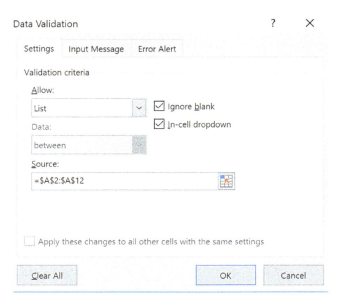

Select OK and your cell will now have a selector arrow and within it will be a list of your students.

Advanced Tools

Multiple or Nested IFs

A multiple IF is a formula based on multiple conditions. Like the IF statement, it is made up of a condition, what we do if that condition is met or true, and what we do if the condition is not met or false. The difference in a multiple IF is that once we have given our first condition and what we would do if it was true we leave out what we would do if it was not true and apply a second condition and result as below:

If, You Keep skipping School, **You are Going to Get Expelled,** IF you stop you can stay in school.

If, You Keep skipping School, **You are Going to Get Expelled, IF** you keep fighting with other students, You are going to get expelled, IF you stop you can stay in school.

So you can add as many conditions and what happens if true as you need by inserting a new **IF** statement after the what happens if true and only once you have finished giving conditions you add the what happens if the condition is not met as below:

If in our previous example, we had a room for each teacher instead of just **Classroom A** and **The Hall** we would need to create a formula like this:

=IF(A2="Teacher 1","Classroom A",IF(A2="Teacher 2","Classroom B","The Hall"))

	A	B	C
1	**Teachers**	**Students**	**Classroom**
2	Teacher 1	Adam	=IF(A2="Teacher 1","Classroom A",IF(A2="Teacher 2","Classroom B","The Hall"))
3	Teacher 1	Bella	
4	Teacher 3	Charles	
5	Teacher 1	Donna	
6	Teacher 3	Etnan	
7	Teacher 2	Fiona	
8	Teacher 3	Michael	
9	Teacher 3	Craig	
10	Teacher 1	Terry	
11	Teacher 3	Katrina	
12	Teacher 2	Mary	

And would produce the following:

	A	B	C
1	**Teachers**	**Students**	**Classroom**
2	Teacher 1	Adam	Classroom A
3	Teacher 1	Bella	Classroom A
4	Teacher 3	Charles	The Hall
5	Teacher 1	Donna	Classroom A
6	Teacher 3	Etnan	The Hall
7	Teacher 2	Fiona	Classroom B
8	Teacher 3	Michael	The Hall
9	Teacher 3	Craig	The Hall
10	Teacher 1	Terry	Classroom A
11	Teacher 3	Katrina	The Hall
12	Teacher 2	Mary	Classroom B

IF/AND Formulas

Where we need an IF formula where two or more conditions *must* be met we would create an IF/AND formula.

Within this formula you need to give the conditions in a separate set of brackets and what happens if true then give what happens if the condition is not true.

In the below table, a student must score greater than 50% in all three exams in order to pass:

	A	B	C	D
1	**Student**	**Exam1**	**Exam2**	**Exam3**
2	Adam	75.00%	80.00%	95.00%
3	Bella	40.00%	55.00%	60.00%
4	Charles	60.00%	65.00%	70.00%
5	Donna	45.00%	49.00%	50.00%
6	Ethan	25.00%	40.00%	65.00%
7	Fiona	51.00%	49.00%	70.00%

Our formula would need to look like this:

IF(AND(B2>50%,C2>50%,C3>50%),**"Pass","Fail")**

So in an IF/AND you list the conditions separated by a comma (the section in blue) and once you have put all of your conditions in you put a closed bracket followed by a comma. You then put the result if *all three* of your conditions are met (the section in red) and then the result if *any* of your conditions are not met (the section in green).

Rank Tie Breakers

For the techniques I use, the rank formula is crucial, however, it brings with it some issues. When you use the rank formula if there is a tie it will give two or more numbers the same rank as below:

	A	B	C
1	Student	Score	Rank
2	Adam	75%	4
3	Bella	40%	8
4	Charles	92%	1
5	Donna	45%	7
6	Etnan	25%	11
7	Fiona	51%	6
8	Michael	33%	9
9	Craig	28%	10
10	Terry	92%	1
11	Katrina	78%	3
12	Mary	54%	5

We can see that as Charles and Terry both have 92%, they are both ranked as number one. Although this is correct, it means that the next ranked student is number three as it has missed out number two as there are two students in first.

Because my formulas will be looking for each number in sequence as there is no number two it will return an error when it looks for the second ranked student. The way to overcome this is with a tie breaker.

A tie breaker will break any tie and ensure that no two students or numbers are ranked the same so one will be first and one will be ranked second even though the number is the same. The popular tie breaker that you will find on your chosen search engine will be the example below:

=Rank(B2,B$2:B$12)+COUNTIF($B$2:B2,B2)-1

	A	B	C
1	**Student**	**Score**	**Rank**
2	Adam	75%	4
3	Bella	40%	8
4	Charles	92%	1
5	Donna	45%	7
6	Etnan	25%	11
7	Fiona	51%	6
8	Michael	33%	9
9	Craig	28%	10
10	Terry	92%	2
11	Katrina	78%	3
12	Mary	54%	5

We now have a separate rank for each student.

IFERROR Formula

Often when we use LOOKUP formulas we will be looking for information that we know is not there. When this happens the formula will return an error.

The IFERROR formula allows us to control what is displayed instead of an error and can be used to wrap any formula. I always found it more useful to complete my formula, check the errors that were displayed and then add the IFERROR so I didn't hide errors that I needed to fix.

The below INDEX MATCH formula will return an error when it looks for Teacher 4 because Teacher 4 does not have a Private Tuition student. As this may not always be the case, we still need to include Teacher 4 in our LOOKUP.

In the table below I want to bring in the private tuition student for each of the teachers, however, when I search for Teacher 4 it will return an error as Teacher 4 does not appear in our list:

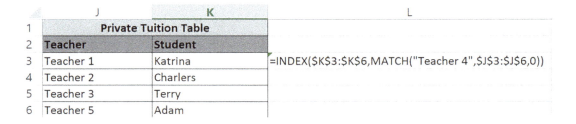

	J	K	L
1	**Private Tuition Table**		
2	**Teacher**	**Student**	
3	Teacher 1	Katrina	=INDEX($K$3:$K$6,MATCH("Teacher 4",$J$3:$J$6,0))
4	Teacher 2	Charlers	
5	Teacher 3	Terry	
6	Teacher 5	Adam	

The result would be the following error code:

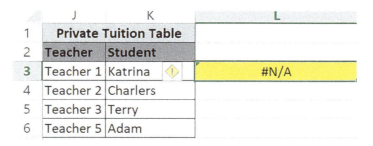

As we do not want the "#N/A" showing on our spreadsheet we can wrap the formula in an IFERROR formula so instead of "#N/A" it will return a number or text of our choice. In this case we have selected for it to return "No Students".

The original formula is :

=INDEX($K$3:$K$6,MATCH("Teacher 4",$J$3:$J$6,0))

The new formula would be:

=**IFERROR(**INDEX($K$3:$K$6,MATCH("Teacher 4",$J$3:$J$6,0))**,"No Students")**

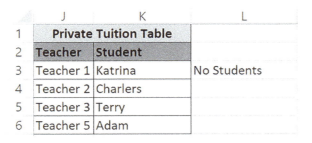

So we can see that we have not amended the original formula, all we have done is put IFERROR and an open bracket at the start "IFERROR(" and a comma and what we want to replace the error with followed by a closed bracket at the end ",No Students"). Remember, if you are replacing the error with a number no speech marks are required.

	J	K	L
1	Private Tuition Table		
2	Teacher	Student	
3	Teacher 1	Katrina	No Students
4	Teacher 2	Charlers	
5	Teacher 3	Terry	
6	Teacher 5	Adam	

This can be applied to *any* formula in the same way.

Index Match Formulas

INDEX MATCH serves the same function as a VLOOKUP but is not restricted to looking left to right.

Index(Range of Data I want to Bring In, **Match**(The Unique Info to Match,The Range of Data to Match it in), 0 for an exact match))

	A	B
1	**Teachers**	**Students**
2	Teacher 1	Adam
3	Teacher 1	Bella
4	Teacher 3	Charles
5	Teacher 1	Donna
6	Teacher 3	Etnan
7	Teacher 2	Fiona
8	Teacher 3	Michael
9	Teacher 3	Craig
10	Teacher 1	Terry
11	Teacher 3	Katrina
12	Teacher 2	Mary

If in the above table we needed to identify the teacher that a particular student had, a VLOOKUP would not work as your result, the teacher would need to be to the right of what you were matching, the student.

But using an INDEX MATCH the result could be either to the left or right of what you were matching.

=Index(A2:A12,MATCH("Fiona",B2:B12,0)

The above formula would find Fiona in column B and bring in the name in the same row as Fiona in column A, "Teacher 2".